The Manager's Pocket Guide to Project Management

Michael Greer

HRD Press ❖ Amherst, MA

Production services by Jean Miller
Cover design by Eileen Klockars
Editorial services by Robie Grant

ISBN 0-87425-488-4

PRINTED IN CANADA

Dedication

For Bonnie, who after 25 years of marriage, continues to challenge, support, and encourage me to be my best.

About the Author

Michael Greer is author of *The Project Manager's Partner: A Step-by-Step Guide to Project Management* (HRD Press, 1996), as well as the Partner's facilitator's guide, *Project Management for Workgroups* (HRD Press, 1997). Greer also wrote the award-winning *ID Project Management: Tools and Techniques for Instructional Designers and Developers* (Educational Technology Publications, 1992). For many years Greer managed teams of contractors as they worked side-by-side with new product developers to create training and performance improvement systems for major corporations. In his role as consultant and PM workshop administrator, Greer has helped many organizations redesign their PM practices. His primary mission is to demystify PM and make it accessible to new and part-time project managers.

For free handouts, a frequently updated PM bibliography, links to PM-related web sites, and other PM information, please visit *Michael Greer's Project Management Resources* website at: **http://michaelgreer.home. mindspring.com**.

For assistance customizing Greer's HRD Press materials for your organization or to schedule a custom-tailored, in-house PM workshop, contact:

Michael Greer
(310) 822-3216 (winter/spring)
(814) 797-2846 (summer/fall)
e-mail: michaelgreer@mindspring.com

Before you begin . . .

As you read this pocket guide, you will notice a number of worksheets. A full-size, electronic version of these worksheets is available through our website for purchasers of this book.

To obtain an electronic copy, contact: http://www.hrdpress.com

The Manager's Pocket Guide to Project Management
Table of Contents

Introduction 1

How to Use This Handbook 3

Part I. Your Deliverables, Phases, and
Project Life Cycle 3

Part II: Your Essential Project Actions 3

Part III: Your Project Management Action
Tools... 4

Where to Begin.. 4

**Part I: Your Deliverables, Phases, and
Project Life Cycle** 7

Project Deliverables 7

Project Phases 8

The Project Life Cycle.................................... 10

Phase I: Determine Need and Feasibility 13

Phase II: Create Project Plan 14

Phase III: Create Specifications for
Deliverables.. 15

Phase IV: Create Deliverables 16

Phase V: Test and Implement Deliverables....... 18

Assignment: Your Unique Project Life Cycle..... 19

Worksheet: My Unique Project Life Cycle 20

Part II: Your Essential Project Actions 25

Project Management Processes 25

    Initiating 28
    Planning 28
    Executing 30
    Controlling 31
    Closing 33

Project Phases and the Project Management Processes 34

Assignment: Your Essential Project Actions 36

Summary of Key Project Manager Actions and Results 37

Phases, Processes, and Action Items: Pulling It All Together 45

Part III: Your Project Management Action Tools 51

Overview 51

    Initiating 52
    Planning 52
    Executing 53
    Controlling 53
    Closing 53

Action Tool: Demonstrate Project Need and Feasibility 54

    Worksheet: Demonstrating Project Need and Feasibility 55

Action Tool: Obtain Project Authorization 58

    Worksheet: Is This Project Authorized? 59
    Worksheet: The Project Charter 61

Action Tool: Obtain Authorization for the Phase 63

    Worksheet: Is This Phase Really
    Authorized? 65

Action Tool: Describe Project Scope 67

    Checklist: Evaluating the Project Scope 68
    Worksheet: Project Scope Statement.........70
    Example: Work Breakdown Structure
    (WBS) 72

Action Tool: Define and Sequence Project Activities 74

    Guidelines for Defining and Sequencing
    Project Activities 75
    Example: Project Network Diagram............77

Action Tool: Estimate Durations for Activities and Resources Required 78

    Guidelines for Estimating Durations for
    Activities and Resources Required...........79
    Worksheet: Estimating Durations for
    Activities and Resources Required...........82

Action Tool: Develop a Project Schedule 84

    Guidelines for Developing the Project
    Schedule 85
    Example: Project Schedules......................90

Action Tool: Estimate Costs 95

    Example: A "Bottom Up" Cost Estimate 96
    Guidelines for Making a "Bottom Up"
    Cost Estimate....................................101

Action Tool: Build a Budget and Spending
Plan 104

   Guidelines for Building a Budget and
     Spending Plan 105

Optional Action Tool: Create a Formal
Quality Plan.. 109

   Guidelines for Creating a Formal
     Quality Plan 110

Optional Action Tool: Create a Formal
Project Communications Plan...................... 112

   Guidelines for Developing the Project
     Communications Plan 113
   Worksheet: Project Communications
     Planner... 116

Action Tool: Organize and Acquire Staff........ 118

   Guidelines for Developing the
     Organizational Plan and Strategy for
     Acquiring Staff.................................. 119
   Worksheet: Project Responsibility/
     Accountability Matrix 124
   Guidelines: Tips for Working with Experts
     Outside Your Area of Expertise.............. 127

Optional Action Tool: Identify Risks and
Plan to Respond... 129

   Guidelines for Identifying Risks and
     Planning to Respond 130
   Worksheet: Risk Assessment and
     Response Analyzer............................. 134

Optional Action Tool: Plan for and Acquire
Outside Resources 136

   Guidelines for Planning to Procure
     Outside Goods or Services 138

Guidelines for Soliciting Bids for
Outside Goods or Services 143
Guidelines for Selecting the Best
Contractor for the Job 145

Action Tool: Organize the Project Plan 149

Guidelines for Creating the Project Plan ... 150

Action Tool: Close Out the Project Planning
Phase 153

Guidelines for Closing Out the Project
Planning Phase 154

Action Tool: Revisit the Project Plan and
Re-plan If Needed 157

Guidelines for Revisiting the Plan and
Re-planning If Needed 158

Action Tool: Execute Project Activities 160

Guidelines for Executing a Project
Phase 162

Action Tool: Control Project Activities 165

Guidelines: Keeping Things Moving—
A "To-Do" List and Tools to Help
You Execute, Control, and Close Out
Your Project 166
Worksheet: Project Deliverables Status
Analyzer 170
Worksheet: Variance Analyzer 172
Guidelines: Handling Scope Change 175
Worksheet: Project Scope Change
Order 178
Worksheet: Project Issue Tracker 180
Worksheet: The Project Status Report 182

Action Tool: Close Out Project Activities 184

   Guidelines for Closing Out a Project or
     Phase.. 185
   Worksheet: Sample Project Sign-Off
     Form.. 189

**Appendix A: Potential Shortcuts for
Low-Risk Projects** A-1

**Appendix B: Guidelines — When to Kill
the Project** B-1

**Appendix C: Glossary of Project
Management Terms** C-1

References R-1

Subject Index I-1

Introduction

This handbook is based on HRD Press' best-selling guide ***The Project Manager's Partner: A Step-by-Step Guide to Project Management.*** Both build upon The Project Management Institute's ***PMBOK*** (Project Management Body of Knowledge), providing specific how-to-do-it tips for achieving many of PMBOK's recommended best practices.

The Manager's Pocket Guide to Project Management is designed as a quick reference guide for the busy manager. All the ***Partner's*** time-tested PM worksheets and guidelines are here, without the extensive theory and background information that enrich the ***Project Manager's Partner***. The Pocket Guide is meant to be a practical reference: The author has drawn on his recent training and consulting experiences using the ***Partner*** to create more than a dozen powerful new project management tools, published here for the first time. These include:

- Worksheet: My Unique Project Life Cycle
- Worksheet: The Project Charter
- Worksheet: Project Scope Statement
- Worksheet: Estimating Durations for Required Activities and Resources

- Worksheet: Project Communications Planner

- Worksheet: Risk Assessment and Response Analyzer

- Guidelines: Keeping Things Moving—A "To-Do" List and Tools to Help You Execute, Control, and Close Out Your Project

- Worksheet: Project Deliverables Status Analyzer

- Worksheet: Variance Analyzer

- Guidelines: Handling Scope Change

- Worksheet: Project Scope Change Order

- Worksheet: Project Issue Tracker

- Worksheet: The Project Status Report

- Worksheet: Sample Project Sign-Off Form

- Guidelines: When to Kill the Project

Please note that all worksheets from *The Manager's Pocket Guide to Project Management* are available in full-size versions. The worksheets are free to purchasers of the book by going to the HRD Press website at http://www.hrdpress.com, and downloading them.

We hope you find this Pocket Guide to be a valuable tool for planning and managing your projects, and that you enjoy the experience!

How to Use This Handbook

This handbook is divided into three major sections. Each major section corresponds to one of the "big picture" chores that most project managers face when setting up and managing a project.

Part I: Your Deliverables, Phases, and Project Life Cycle

This part of the handbook will help you complete your first big chore: Figuring out your *project life cycle*—in particular, figuring out how your project's major *deliverables (results)* will determine your appropriate *project phases,* and how these phases can be grouped together to make up the *life cycle* of your project. This section presents a generic project life cycle, along with a tool and suggestions that will help you develop your own customized project life cycle.

Part II: Your Essential Project Actions

This part of the handbook will help you complete your second big chore: Figuring out which *actions* you need to take to complete your project. In other words, given the phases and life cycle you identified in Part I, what actions must you take to get the project done effectively? This section provides a list of project management best practices from which you can select those most applicable to your project.

Part III: Your Project Management Action Tools

This part of the handbook will help you complete your third big chore: Figuring out what specific steps to take to accomplish your essential project management actions. This is the heart of the handbook. It contains *tools* in the form of worksheets, guidelines, and check-lists to help guide you through each of the actions you identified as important in Part II. While you won't need to use every tool for every project, you are likely to find that these tools contain valuable solutions to many of your typical project problems.

Where to Begin

The table on the following page will help you figure out where to begin.

If . . .	*Then . . .*
You are a new project manager working on your first project . . .	Work through Parts I and II; then refer to appropriate sections of Part III, as needed.
You are a first-time project manager working in an organization that has clearly prescribed for you your project's deliverables, phases, and project life cycles . . .	Skim through Part I and try to relate your organization's phases and life cycle to those presented in the text. Then work through Part II and appropriate sections of Part III.
You are an experienced project manager who is clear about your project's deliverables, phases, and appropriate life cycle . . .	Skip Part I. Skim through Part II and move on to appropriate sections of Part III.
You have a lot of experience managing projects, but would like an informational review . . .	Skim through all sections of the handbook and challenge yourself by trying to apply the concepts to your company's procedures.

Part I: Your Deliverables, Phases, and Project Life Cycle

A ***project*** is a ***temporary endeavor undertaken to create a unique product or service***.[1] Because projects by definition are temporary, project managers must get their projects completed by expending only the amount of time, money, labor, and other resources that have been allocated. In addition, because projects result in unique products or services (deliverables), projects are typically organized into specific phases that most appropriately reflect the evolution of these unique deliverables. These project phases, taken as a whole, make up the overall life cycle of the project. Everything is inextricably linked: the deliverables of your project, the project's phases, and your project's life cycle. Let's look at each of these.

Project Deliverables

By ***deliverables*** we are referring to ***any measurable, tangible, verifiable output that must be produced to complete the project***.[2] These may include ***interim deliverables*** (like scripts, system specifications, or blueprints) and ***finished deliverables*** (like the finished motion picture, the software package, or the

7

completed building). Let's say you are creating a new product that will help your organization obtain a larger market share and greater profits. The deliverables for your project might include the following:

- An analysis of the market, describing where your new product will fit in among its competitors and what specific needs it will meet in the marketplace

- A feasibility study detailing how your organization will be able to design, manufacture, and distribute the new product

- A description of the overall project concept

- A detailed project plan

- Product specifications (blueprints, flow-charts, etc.)

- A prototype or mock-up of the new product

- Tests of the new product, using members of the product's target audience or buyers

- Enhancements or revisions to the new product based on the test results

Project Phases

A **project phase** is a *collection of project activities, usually resulting in the creation of a major deliverable.*[3] Consider the list of deliverables above. There are literally hundreds of project activities that must be undertaken in order to create all the deliverables listed. We could jump right in and try to complete all of these activities at once, but this would likely result in chaos. Instead, we combine the activities into clusters and sequence them so that we can proceed logically and systematically. In short, we group the project activities into phases. To continue our example, here are some appropriate project phases that would systematically yield the deliverables from our example above:

- *Phase I: Determine Need and Feasibility*—In this phase we complete all the detailed analysis work, including the market analysis, feasibility study, and overall project concept.

- *Phase II: Create Project Plan*—In this phase, after the need and feasibility are approved, we complete all the activities necessary to create a detailed plan for the rest of the project.

- *Phase III: Create Product Specifications*—In this phase, we create detailed product blueprints, flowcharts, and so on. These should be reviewed by outside experts and managers, and then revised as needed.

- **Phase IV: Create Prototype Product**—In this phase, we complete all the activities necessary to create our prototype or mock up.

- **Phase V: Test and Implement**—In this phase we organize and conduct tests, make enhancements and revisions, and finalize the product.

Notice that our project phases are logically related to the deliverables we are creating. Within the phases, the deliverables evolve gradually and in successive approximations. In particular, the phases build in plenty of opportunity for project players to review results and make changes before too much time and money are spent.

The Project Life Cycle

The **project life cycle** is a *collection of project phases whose name and number are determined by the control needs of the organization involved in the project.*[4] For example, the five-phased sample project life cycle just described affords plenty of opportunity for control by the sponsoring organization. At the end of each phase the project can be reviewed and deliverables revised, or the entire project can be stopped. In this way the organization protects its investment.

Because the types of deliverables resulting from projects differ widely from one industry to another, the project controls and phases used also can be quite different. For example, most film production projects include an editing or post-production phase, while most homebuilding projects include a blueprint phase.

Different deliverables evolve in different ways, requiring different project phases. Yet no matter what the industry, **stakeholders** (i.e., those who are affected by project activities)[5] review and approve deliverables at each phase before allowing the next phase to begin. In this way, stakeholders try to ensure that deliverables evolve in a steady, controlled fashion and that resources are not wasted.

As an industry matures, its typical project life cycles come to represent industry-wide "best practices." By using an industry-standard project life cycle, project managers can make certain that deliverables conform to recognized quality standards, and that the project schedule and budget will be maintained. What's more, when you compare your project to the industry standard, you can quickly identify how your project will differ. This allows you to isolate activities that require especially thorough analysis and planning.

However, you may at some point find yourself in charge of planning and managing a project that doesn't seem to fit one of the industry-specific life cycles. In such situations, you can apply our Generic Project Life Cycle. It incorporates phases and activities that we believe are nearly universal in their application. The five phases of the Generic Project Life Cycle are illustrated in the diagram that follows:

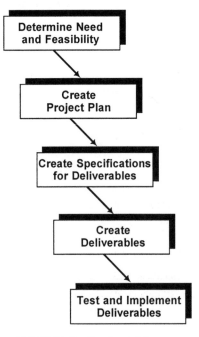

FIGURE 1. Project Phases

Let's briefly examine each of these phases:

Phase I: Determine Need and Feasibility

In this phase, the project manager and application specialists attempt to confirm that there is a need for the project deliverables. In addition, they try to decide whether the project is "doable"—that is, whether it is possible to plan and execute a project to create these deliverables.

Activities

Activities that should be undertaken during this phase include, but are not limited to, the following:

- Goal definition
- Concept definition
- Needs analysis
- Market analysis
- Strategy definition
- Preliminary benefit/cost analysis.[6]

This phase culminates in a formal approval of the project concept or a "go/no go" decision.

Phase II: Create Project Plan

Because projects are of finite duration and sometimes use unique work processes, the planning of a project is particularly important. In this phase, the project manager and/or application specialists create a formal document to guide the project team as they execute the project.

Activities

Activities that should be undertaken during this phase include:

- Creating a formal planning document that may be used to:
  - Link project activities to expressed needs and feasibility studies (i.e., tying the plan to the outputs of Phase I: Determine Need and Feasibility)
  - Provide a written record of assumptions regarding deliverables, work processes, resources required, and so forth
  - Help communicate clearly with stakeholders
  - Provide a written record of agreed-upon scope, costs, and schedule
  - Facilitate a critique of project assumptions held by stakeholders

• Getting the project plan approved by sponsors and other stakeholders before project work begins.[7]

Phase III: Create Specifications for Deliverables

In this phase, application specialists create a formal document that describes in substantial detail the deliverables that are to be created. Examples of such detailed specifications include:

• Software design documents
• Blueprints for a building
• A detailed media treatment for a videotape production

It's important to distinguish the extensive Phase III deliverables specifications from the preliminary specifications created as part of the Phase II planning process. In the Phase II planning process, the project team describes the deliverables in just enough detail to create a project plan. Once the plan is approved, the project team can begin spending resources (including time and money) on the project. It makes good business sense to wait until Phase III to extend the preliminary specifications. At this time, they should be "fleshed out" substantially so that project stakeholders can evaluate them at length. In this way, the project team can make written modifications instead of reworking the deliverables.

Note: These detailed specifications some-times identify unanticipated deliverables. Therefore, this phase often includes descriptions of ways in which schedules or budgets need to be refined, as well as new project assumptions.

Activities

Activities that should be undertaken during this phase include:

- Creating one or more documents describing the specifications of all deliverables in substantial detail
- Obtaining approval of the specifications from sponsors and other stakeholders.[8]

Phase IV: Create Deliverables

The most time-consuming and resource-intensive phase of the project is usually the phase in which the project deliverables are created according to the approved deliverable specifications. In other words, to extend our Phase III examples, the software is developed, the building is built, the videotape is produced, and so on.

The specific activities involved in this phase differ dramatically from one industry or application to another. For example, a defense contractor may first need to create a working model to prove that the concept works before building the full-blown version of the defense system. And a software developer will likely create and test small units of code before programming and integrating all software modules. A video producer would likely create scripts, conduct casting sessions and rehearsals, and produce other interim deliverables prior to engaging in full-blown production activities.

Activities

Activities that should be undertaken during this phase include, but are by no means limited to, the following:

- Creating prototypes of deliverables
- Creating portions or pieces of deliverables
- Providing services as promised in the project plan
- Completing fully integrated deliverables
- Obtaining sponsor and other stakeholder approval for each deliverable or service, as appropriate.[9]

Phase V: Test and Implement Deliverables

In this phase, the project deliverables are shown to work as planned and are turned over to the sponsor or customer for use. As in Phase IV, the specific activities involved in this phase differ dramatically from one industry or application to another. The defense contractor will likely test and refine the product and manufacturing processes many times before going into full production and deployment. The software producer is likely to run user tests and make revisions prior to delivery to the customer. And the video producer may conduct audience tests of "rough cuts" prior to final editing and delivery to the client.

Activities

Activities that should be undertaken during this phase include, but are certainly not limited to, the following:

- Testing of deliverables, together or in part

- Refinement of deliverables based on test results

- Implementation of deliverables on a limited basis (such as a field trial)

- Further refinement of deliverables based on preliminary implementation

- Full production of final deliverables

- Sponsor or other stakeholder approval of test results, resulting plans for modification of deliverables, and final deliverables.[10]

Assignment: Your Unique Project Life Cycle

Bearing in mind your project's unique deliverables, use the worksheet that follows to determine your project's unique phases and life cycles.

Worksheet: My Unique Project Life Cycle

Instructions: This tool will help you to create your own custom-tailored project life cycle — one that best reflects the unique requirements of your project's deliverables and your organization. Refer to the first two columns as your "crib sheet," then fill in the third column with between 3 and 7 broad phases which your project should employ. In the last column, note the key activities that will be essential to the success of each phase. (Continue on the back of the page, if necessary.)

Typical Project Phases	Typical Project Activities	My Project's Phases	My Project's Activities
Determine Need and Feasibility *Purpose:* Confirm that project is needed, do-able; formal "go/no go" approval.	• Goal and concept definition • Needs or market analysis • Strategy definition • Preliminary benefit/cost analysis		

Continued . . . .

Typical Project Phases	Typical Project Activities	My Project's Phases	My Project's Activities
Create Project Plan *Purpose:* Create formal document to guide project team as it executes project.	• Involve stakeholders in specifying and agreeing on project outcomes and methodology • Create written record of assumptions, agreed-upon scope, resources, schedule, costs, etc. • Obtain consensus and formal approval		

Continued . . . .

Typical Project Phases	Typical Project Activities	My Project's Phases	My Project's Activities
Create Specifications for Deliverables *Purpose:* Describe deliverables in substantial detail "on paper."	• Create design plans, flowcharts, blueprints, media treatments, other "on paper" deliverables; descriptions and samples as appropriate • Circulate and obtain feedback, revise, obtain formal approval		

Continued . . . .

22

Typical Project Phases	Typical Project Activities	My Project's Phases	My Project's Activities
Create Deliverables *Purpose:* Create prototypes, pieces; create full-blown, fully integrated deliverables.	• Create all promised deliverables, in "chunks" or completely • Provide planned services, execute planned activities, obtain formal approval		

23

Continued . . .

Typical Project Phases	Typical Project Activities	My Project's Phases	My Project's Activities
Test and Implement Deliverables *Purpose:* Make sure project deliverables work as planned; turn over to sponsor for use.	• Testing of deliverables (in whole or in part) • Refinement, revision • Full production, implementation, and final approval		

Concluded

Part II: Your Essential Project Actions

Given the deliverables and phases you identified in Part I, what actions must you take to get the project done effectively? This section provides a review of essential project management (PM) *processes* as identified in the Project Management Institute's PMBOK (Project Management Body of Knowledge).[11] In addition, we provide a list of *essential PM actions* derived from those processes, from which you may select those most applicable to your project.

Project Management Processes

In Part I we identified three important *whats* related to the project:

- What are the deliverables to be created?
- What are the phases we will use to organize the project?
- What is our overall project life cycle?

Now it's time to consider some of the *hows* related to the project:

- How will we move from phase to phase within the project?

- How should the project manager determine specific assignments and "to dos" for the project team?

- In short, how will we take action to complete the project?

The answers to these "how" questions may be found by examining the essential project management processes.

A **process** can be defined as *a series of actions designed to bring about specific results.*[12] There are five processes that should be applied to *each phase* of a project in order to bring about the completion of the phase. These processes are listed below:

- Initiating
- Planning
- Executing
- Controlling
- Closing

Three of these processes (planning, executing, and controlling) apply to any type of management activity, whether it involves a project or an ongoing operation.[13] Since projects are temporary (i.e., they have an identifiable starting point and require timely completion), they must also include the processes of initiating (starting up) and closing (formally accepting the results and ending the phase).[14]

Note that all of these processes eventually become unconscious habits of effective project managers. If you start out consciously practicing them, they'll eventually be internalized and you will begin to move among them in a fluid way, helping to ensure your project's success.

The diagram shown below illustrates how these project management processes are linked together.

Let's take a closer look at each of these processes.

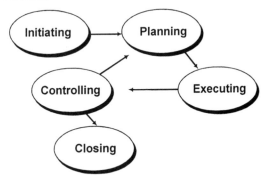

FIGURE 2: Project Management Processes[15]

Initiating

Initiating means getting the project authorized. It involves obtaining the organization's commitment to the project as a whole. Alternately, initiating can involve getting the organization's commitment that a particular project phase should be started.[16]

Typically, the sponsor, customer, or person providing the funds gives the authorization to begin a project or phase. So, in effect, initiating means getting the "green light" from the client to begin work.

Planning

Planning is of major importance because by definition the project involves creating something unique.[17] In other words, you may be heading into uncharted waters, so you should have a plan to help you get through them safely. There are two types of planning: *essential* planning and *discretionary* planning.

Essential Planning

Essential planning consists of these four subprocesses:

- Defining the scope (all the products and services to be provided by the project)
- Identifying or defining the required activities, resources, and schedule

- Creating detailed cost estimates and budgets

- Integrating all of the above into a comprehensive project plan

We call these subprocesses "essential" because no one should undertake a project or project phase without first completing all four of them. [18]

Discretionary Planning

Discretionary planning processes are desirable, but they are not necessarily required to complete a project.[19] These processes are performed as needed and might include the creation of formal plans such as these:

- Quality plan
- Communications plan
- Staffing plan (over and above what is described in the essential plan above)
- Procurement plan
- Risk assessment/response plan
- Other formal plans dictated by organizational values and policies

Some veteran project managers will no doubt argue that adopting one or more of these plans is not discretionary, but essential.

Depending on your organization and your industry, you may agree. You should at least quickly skim through the Action Tool associated with each of these planning processes and decide whether it might apply to your project; if it clearly does not apply, then reject it. In this way, you will be sure that you have done your job as project manager by challenging all assumptions about the work process, selecting the best possible approaches, and taking nothing for granted.

In any case, whether you classify the particular outputs as essential or discretionary, planning is a vital process of project management. As you will see in Part III, the majority of the Action Tools in this handbook are designed to support the planning process.

Executing

Executing is the process by which project plans are carried out. Executing involves several subprocesses:

- **Project Plan Execution**—carrying out the project plan as written. Specifically, project plan execution involves building the house, producing the motion picture, developing the new software, or carrying out whatever activities the plan calls for.[20]

- **Team Development**—developing individual and group skills to enhance project performance. This can include formal and informal training, coaching, and so on.

- **Information Distribution**—making needed information available to project stakeholders in a timely manner.

- **Solicitation**—obtaining quotations, bids, offers, or proposals from contractors, vendors, or other providers of essential goods or services.

- **Source Selection**—choosing from among potential contractors, vendors, or providers.

- **Contract Administration**—managing the relationship with the contractor, vendor, or other provider. This includes such activities as handling paperwork and ensuring payment.

Controlling

Controlling involves comparing actual performance with planned performance. In other words, are you doing exactly what you planned to do? If you discover deviations from the plan (often called "variances"), you must analyze these variances and figure out alternative actions that will get the project back on track. You can then decide which alternative is best and take appropriate corrective action.[21] Controlling involves several subprocesses:

- **Progress Reporting**—collecting and disseminating progress information to all project stakeholders.

- **Overall Change Control**—coordinating changes across the entire project.

- **Scope Change Control**—controlling any changes to the project scope. This often means limiting the project's deliverables to only those that have been planned.

- **Cost Control**—controlling changes to the project budget.

- **Quality Control**—monitoring specific project results to determine if they comply with relevant quality standards, and identifying ways to eliminate causes of unsatisfactory performance.

- **Quality Assurance**—evaluating overall project performance on a regular basis to ensure that the project will meet the relevant quality standards.

- **Risk Control**—attempting to minimize the effect that "unknowns" or potentially negative events will have on the project.[22]

Closing

Because projects are temporary endeavors, projects and project phases must eventually come to an end. But who is to say when a project or phase has ended? More importantly, how do you know when to stop expending effort and money on a project or project phase?

Projects typically involve many stakeholders, each of whom is likely to have an opinion about the suitability of deliverables. To help prevent disputes, you will have to set up a formal process by which the project or project phase may be declared officially completed. This formal process is called *closing*. Closing involves formally accepting the results and ending the project or phase. This includes several subprocesses:

- **Scope Verification**—ensuring that all identified project deliverables have been completely satisfied.

- **Administrative Closure**—generating, gathering, and disseminating information to formalize project completion. You will probably have to "sign-off" or gain written approval of the deliverables or phase.

- **Contract Close-Out**—completion and settlement of the contract, including resolution of any outstanding items.[23]

Note: Clear-cut and effective closing is based on the formal project plan. The project plan should spell out exactly what the deliverables will look like, how and by whom the deliverables will be approved, and so on. By formally agreeing to the plan, the stakeholders have, in advance, agreed to specific deliverables to be created by specific methods. In this way, the finished results can be compared to the planned results, thus minimizing disputes over whether the deliverables are suitable.

Project Phases and the Project Management Processes

The life cycle of a project and the processes used to manage the project are distinct and separate, yet inextricably linked. The project manager uses the processes in order to complete each phase of the life cycle. The diagram that follows illustrates how the phases and processes interrelate.

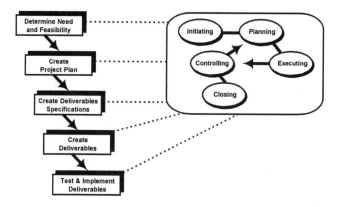

**FIGURE 3. Project Phases and the
Project Management Processes**

Note that the project life cycle is essentially
linear: Each phase results in a work product
that is passed on to the next phase. The
project deliverables evolve gradually,
culminating in the finished product.

On the other hand, the project management
processes are non-linear. They recur over and
over again throughout the project, in all phases.

The project life cycle influences the final
deliverables by identifying the essential outputs
of each phase. In contrast, the project
management processes direct the project
manager in that they identify the actions that
he or she must take to help make the project a
success.

Assignment: Your Essential Project Actions

Bearing in mind your project's unique deliverables, phases, and life cycle, use the guide on the next several pages to help you determine the essential actions you must take as project manager to complete your project.

Summary of Key Project Manager Actions and Results

Below is a list of actions that project managers should take in order to successfully complete a project. Beside each action is a description of one or more specific results that the action should produce. Place a check mark (✓) beside each action and result that will be essential to your project's success.

INITIATING

ACTION	RESULTS OF SUCCESSFUL PERFORMANCE
1. Demonstrate Project Need and Feasibility	• A document confirming that there is a need for the project deliverables and describing, in broad terms: the deliverables; the means of creating the deliverables; the costs of creating and implementing the deliverables; and the benefits to be obtained by implementing the deliverables.

Continued . . .

ACTION	RESULTS OF SUCCESSFUL PERFORMANCE

2. Obtain Project Authorization	• A "go/no go" decision is made by the sponsor
	• A project manager is assigned
	• A "project charter" is created that:
	  – formally recognizes the project
	  – is issued by a manager external to the project and at a high enough organizational level to meet project needs
	  – authorizes the project manager to apply resources to project activities

3. Obtain Authorization for the Phase	• A "go/no go" decision is made by the sponsor that authorizes the project manager to apply organizational resources to the activities of a particular phase
	• Written approval of the phase is obtained that:
	  – formally recognizes the existence of the phase
	  – is issued by a manager external to the project and at a high enough organizational level to meet project needs

Continued . . .

PLANNING

	ACTION	RESULTS OF SUCCESSFUL PERFORMANCE
4.	Describe Project Scope	• Statement of project scope • Scope management plan • Work breakdown structure (WBS)
5.	Define and Sequence Project Activities	• An activity list (list of all activities that will be performed on the project) • Updates to the work breakdown structure (WBS) • A project network diagram
6.	Estimate Durations for Activities and Resources Required	• Estimate of duration (time required) for each activity and assumptions related to each estimate • Statement of resource requirements • Updates to activity list

Continued . . .

ACTION	RESULTS OF SUCCESSFUL PERFORMANCE
7. Develop a Project Schedule	• Project schedule in the form of Gantt charts, network diagrams, milestone charts, or text tables • Supporting details, such as resource usage over time, cash flow projections, order/delivery schedules, etc.
8. Estimate Costs	• Cost estimates for completing each activity • Supporting details, including assumptions and constraints • Cost management plan that describes how cost variances will be handled
9. Build a Budget and Spending Plan	• A cost baseline or time-phased budget for measuring/monitoring costs • A spending plan that tells how much will be spent on what resources, at what time
10. (Optional): Create a Formal Quality Plan	• Quality management plan, including operational definitions • Quality verification checklists

Continued . . .

ACTION	RESULTS OF SUCCESSFUL PERFORMANCE

11. **(Optional):** Create a Formal Project Communications Plan	• A communication management plan, including:
	  – Collection structure
	  – Distribution structure
	  – Description of information to be disseminated
	  – Schedules listing when information will be produced
	  – A method for updating the communications plan

12. Organize and Acquire Staff	• Role and assignments of responsibility • Staffing plan • Organizational chart, with details (as appropriate) • Project staff • Project team directory
13. **(Optional):** Identify Risks and Plan to Respond	• A document describing potential risks, including their sources, symptoms, and ways to address them

Continued . . . .

ACTION	RESULTS OF SUCCESSFUL PERFORMANCE
14. **(Optional)**: Plan for and Acquire Outside Resources	• Procurement management plan describing how contractors will be obtained • Statement of work (SOW) or statement of requirements (SOR) describing the item (product or service) to be procured • Bid documents, such as an RFP (request for proposal), an IFB (invitation for bid), etc. • Evaluation criteria—means of scoring contractor's proposals • Contract with one or more suppliers of goods or services
15. Organize the Project Plan	• A comprehensive project plan that pulls together all the outputs of the preceding project planning activities
16. Close Out the Project Planning Phase	• A project plan that has been approved, in writing, by the sponsor • A "green light" or permission to begin work on the project

Continued . . .

ACTION	RESULTS OF SUCCESSFUL PERFORMANCE
17. Revisit the Project Plan and Re-plan, if Needed	• Assurance or confirmation that the detailed plans to execute a particular phase are still accurate and will effectively achieve the results as planned
EXECUTING	
18. Execute Project Activities	• Work results (deliverables) are created • Change requests (i.e., based on expanded or contracted project) are identified • Periodic progress reports are created • Team performance is assessed, guided, and perhaps improved • Bids/proposals for deliverables are solicited, contractors (suppliers) are chosen, and contracts are established • Contracts are administered to achieve desired work results

Continued . . . .

	CONTROLLING	
ACTION	RESULTS OF SUCCESSFUL PERFORMANCE	
19. Control Project Activities	• Decision to accept inspected deliverables • Corrective actions such as rework of deliverables, adjustments to work processes, etc. • Updates to project plan and scope • List of lessons learned • Improved quality • Completed evaluation checklists (if applicable)	
	CLOSING	
20. Close Out Project Activities	• Formal acceptance, documented in writing, that the sponsor has accepted the product of this phase or activity • Formal acceptance of contractor work products and updates to the contractor's files • Updated project records prepared for archiving • A plan for follow-up and/or hand-off of work products	

Concluded

44

Phases, Processes, and Action Items: Pulling It All Together

So far, we have described five generic project phases that can be used as a baseline to organize nearly any project. In addition, we have described five processes that project managers need to perform in order to complete these project phases.

But how do these elements fit together? The following table makes the connections clear. Here's how to use it:

1. Figure out which phase your project is in (refer to the left column).

2. Decide which project management processes you need to complete (refer to the middle column).

3. Identify the relevant Action Tools that can help you perform the process (refer to the right column).

4. Turn to Part III and locate the relevant Action Tools.

5. Skim through them and decide how you can put them to work for you. Make additions or deletions as appropriate to accommodate your particular industry or organization.

IF... You are in this generic project phase	...AND You want to perform this process	...THEN Refer to these Action Tools
Phase I: Determine Need and Feasibility *(Define goals, concept; analyze need, market; define strategy; do benefit/cost analysis)*	Initiating Phase I Planning Phase I Executing Phase I Controlling Phase I Closing Phase I	• Demonstrate Project Need and Feasibility • Obtain Project Authorization
Phase II: Create Project Plan *(Make a record of all planned deliverables, work processes, resources, scope, etc., and get it approved)*	Initiating Phase II	• Obtain Authorization for the Phase
	Planning Phase II Executing Phase II Controlling Phase II	• Describe Project Scope • Define and Sequence Project Activities • Estimate Durations for Activities and Resources Required

Continued . . .

		• Develop a Project Schedule • Estimate Costs • Build a Budget and Spending Plan • **(Optional)**: Create a Formal Quality Plan • **(Optional)**: Create a Formal Project Communications Plan • Organize and Acquire Staff • **(Optional)**: Identify Risks and Plan to Respond • **(Optional)**: Plan for and Acquire Outside Resources
	Closing Phase II	• Organize the Project Plan • Close Out the Project Planning Phase

47

Continued . . .

Phase III: Create Specifications for Deliverables *(Describe deliverables in detail; get description approved)*	Initiating Phase III	• Obtain Authorization for the Phase
	Planning Phase III	• Revisit the Project Plan and Re-plan, if Needed
	Executing Phase III	• Execute Project Activities
	Controlling Phase III	• Control Project Activities
	Closing Phase III	• Close Out Project Activities
Phase IV: Create Deliverables *(Create prototype pieces; create full-blown, fully integrated deliverables; get them approved)*	Initiating Phase IV	• Obtain Authorization for the Phase
	Planning Phase IV	• Revisit the Project Plan and Re-plan, if Needed
	Executing Phase IV	• Execute Project Activities
	Controlling Phase IV	• Control Project Activities
	Closing Phase IV	• Close Out Project Activities

Continued . . .

Phase V: Test and Implement Deliverables *(Test, refine, produce, and install deliverables)*	Initiating Phase V	• Obtain Authorization for Phase
	Planning Phase V	• Revisit the Project Plan and Re-plan, if Needed
	Executing Phase V	• Execute Project Activities
	Controlling Phase V	• Control Project Activities
	Closing Phase V	• Close Out the Project Activities

Concluded

Part III: Your Project Management Action Tools

This section contains *tools* in the form of worksheets, guidelines, and checklists to help you complete each of the actions you identified as important in Part II. While you won't need to use every tool for every project, you are likely to find that these tools contain valuable solutions to most of your typical project problems.

Overview

This section provides specific tools to help you work through each of the five project management processes. Specifically, these processes are:

- Initiating
- Planning
- Executing
- Controlling
- Closing

(For detailed explanations of these processes, see Part II: Your Essential Project Actions.)

Each Action Tool is divided into these sections:

- *Assignment*—a description of the assignment or specific project management task that this Action Tool will support.

- *Desired Outputs*—the results that should be achieved when you complete this Action Tool.

- *Worksheet and/or Guidelines*—a set of step-by-step procedures to guide you through the completion of the Action Tool.

Below is a list of all the Action Tools. Note that they are organized according to the project management process they support.

Initiating
- *Action Tool:* Demonstrate Project Need and Feasibility

- *Action Tool:* Obtain Project Authorization

- *Action Tool:* Obtain Authorization for the Phase

Planning
- *Action Tool:* Describe Project Scope

- *Action Tool:* Define and Sequence Project Activities

- *Action Tool:* Estimate Durations for Activities and Resources Required

- *Action Tool:* Develop a Project Schedule

- *Action Tool:* Estimate Costs

- *Action Tool:* Build a Budget and Spending Plan

- *Optional Action Tool:* Create a Formal Quality Plan

- *Optional Action Tool:* Create a Formal Project Communications Plan

- *Action Tool:* Organize and Acquire Staff

- *Optional Action Tool:* Identify Risks and Plan to Respond

- *Optional Action Tool:* Plan for and Acquire Outside Resources

- *Action Tool:* Organize the Project Plan

- *Action Tool:* Close Out the Project Planning Phase

- *Action Tool:* Revisit the Project Plan and Re-plan, If Needed

Executing
- *Action Tool:* Execute Project Activities

Controlling
- *Action Tool:* Control Project Activities

Closing
- *Action Tool:* Close Out Project Activities

Action Tool: Demonstrate Project Need and Feasibility

Assignment

Decide whether you have enough information to prove to the sponsor that the project is needed and feasible.

Desired Outputs

- A document confirming that there is a need for the project deliverables; this would include *broad* descriptions of the following items:

  - The project goal and/or underlying concepts

  - The deliverables

  - By what means the deliverables might be created

  - The costs of creating and implementing the deliverables

  - The benefits to be obtained by implementing the deliverables

  - A list of the sponsors and stakeholders

  - In what ways the sponsors and stakeholders are prepared to support the project

Worksheet: Demonstrating Project Need and Feasibility

Instructions: This worksheet is designed to help you decide whether you've "done your homework" and obtained enough information to prove to your sponsor* that the project you propose is needed and is feasible.

Evaluate your project documentation to date by asking yourself each of these questions. (Alternately, you might have a colleague or project supporter review the document with the sponsor's point of view in mind.) Check *Yes* for those questions that you have answered adequately. If you check *No*, review the follow-up suggestion and figure out what to do next.

YES	NO	QUESTIONS
❏	❏	Have I defined the project goal clearly, in terms that the sponsor* can understand? *If not, redefine the goal statement and have it checked by someone who "thinks like the sponsor."*
❏	❏	Is the sponsor financially and organizationally able to provide all needed support? *If not, who is the real sponsor and how can we get the real sponsor involved?*

YES	NO	QUESTIONS
❏	❏	Have I expressed the core project concept clearly and succinctly? *If not, redefine the core project description and have it checked by someone who thinks like the sponsor.*
❏	❏	Does a market analysis or needs analysis show a bona fide need for the product (deliverables) of the project? *If not, consider abandoning the project or conducting an appropriate analysis that proves project need.*
❏	❏	Have we clearly expressed the costs and benefits of the project? *If not, restate the description of costs and benefits and have it checked by someone who thinks like the sponsor.*
❏	❏	Have I consulted all project stakeholders to obtain their opinions about the need and feasibility? *If not, identify missing stakeholders and review the need/feasibility with them, asking for feedback.*
❏	❏	Have we defined a project strategy in enough detail to enable the sponsors to really understand what they're getting into? *If not, restate the project strategy and have it checked by someone who thinks like the sponsor.*

YES	NO	QUESTIONS
❑	❑	Have I assembled the results of my research into a well-written document and/or presentation? *If not, create your document or presentation and have it checked by someone who thinks like the sponsor.*
❑	❑	Have I identified an appropriate audience and scheduled a time, place, and date for presenting my project proposal? *If not, discuss these items with your supervisor (or a more experienced project manager) and figure out what to do next.*
❑	❑	Have I rehearsed the presentation, including my answers to potentially controversial questions? *If not, plan and conduct such a rehearsal.*

Sponsor is the customer, client, final owner, or entity providing funding. The sponsor has the power to provide funds, approve the use of resources, and/or stop the project.

Action Tool: Obtain Project Authorization ☑️

Assignment

Obtain suitable authorization from the sponsor to begin the project.

Desired Outputs

- A "go/no go" decision is made by the sponsor.

  If *"no go,"* all planning typically stops.

  If *"go,"* the next items apply.

- A project manager is identified and assigned.[24]

- A "project charter" is created that:

  - Formally recognizes the existence of the project;

  - Is supported by a manager external to the project and at a high enough organizational level so that he or she can support project needs;

  - Authorizes the project manager to apply organizational resources (people, equipment, materials) to project activities. [25]

Worksheet: Is This Project Authorized?

Instructions: This worksheet will help you figure out whether you have been fully authorized to continue with the project you proposed. Assuming that you have been given some form of approval to begin the project, evaluate that approval to determine if it provides you with the authority you need in order to do the job. (*If you are working with a formal or informal advisory group, you might ask its members to complete this worksheet for you.*)

YES	NO	QUESTIONS
❏	❏	Has the project been formally recognized as a project by one or more sponsors? *If not, find out why and discuss what to do next with your supervisor or the potential sponsor.*
❏	❏	Has news of the project been widely circulated in written form? *If not, find out why and figure out what to do next.*
❏	❏	Has project authorization been issued by a manager external to the project and at a high enough organizational level to help meet project needs? *If not, identify an appropriate sponsoring manager and figure out how you can get his or her authorization.*

YES	NO	QUESTIONS
❏	❏	Has the project manager been identified? *If not, find out who should appoint the project manager and what steps are needed to get the project manager officially on board.*
❏	❏	Is the project manager authorized to apply organizational resources (people, equipment, materials) to project activities? *If the project manager has not been formally authorized, then ask the sponsor by whose authority project resources will be applied.*
❏	❏	Has the project manager been given the green light to move on to the next project phase? *If not, decide what conditions need to be met to get authorization, and begin to meet them.*
❏	❏	Has a project charter been created and approved by appropriate decision makers? *If not, create one and get it approved. (See Worksheet: The Project Charter)*

Remember: If the project isn't authorized, you probably should not be expending resources (including your own time) working on it.

Worksheet: The Project Charter

Project Name: _____ **Date:**_____

Project Manager:_____

Project Tracking No.: _____

Project Justification (Problem or Opportunity Addressed):

Overview of Deliverables (high-level, broad-brush only—provide any details in appendices):

Specific Project Objectives and Success Criteria (schedule, cost, quality):

Primary Stakeholders and Roles (including a broad statement of the roles and responsibilities of all customers, sponsors, contributors, reviewers, managers, sign-off authorities, project managers, etc.):

Key Assumptions:

Signatures—The following people agree that the above information is accurate:

- Project team members:

- Project sponsor and/or authorizing manager(s):

Action Tool: Obtain Authorization for the Phase ☑️

Note: The need for authorization to begin each phase will depend on the type of project and the organizations involved. Initial approval of the entire project may be enough to initiate authorization of each project phase automatically.

Assignment

Obtain suitable authorization from the sponsor to begin a particular project phase.

Desired Outputs

- A *"go/no go"* decision is made by the sponsor concerning whether the project manager will be authorized to apply organizational resources (people, equipment, materials) to the activities of a particular phase (as opposed to the entire project).

  - If *"no go,"* all work typically stops.

  - If *"go,"* continue with the next items.

- Written approval for the phase does the following:

  - Formally recognizes the existence of the phase;

63

- Is supported by a manager external to the project and at a high enough organizational level so that he or she can support the needs of the phase;

- Authorizes the project manager to apply organizational resources (people, equipment, materials) to activities of the phase. [26]

Worksheet: Is This Phase Really Authorized?

Instructions: This worksheet will help you figure out whether you have been fully authorized to begin a project phase. Assuming that you have been given some form of approval to begin the phase, evaluate that approval to determine if it provides you with the authority you need to do the job. (*If you are working with a formal or informal advisory group, you might ask its members to complete this worksheet with you.*)

YES	NO	QUESTIONS
❑	❑	Is the phase we are about to begin part of a project that has been formally recognized as a project? *If not, return to Action Item: Obtain Project Authorization.*
❑	❑	Have all appropriate stakeholders approved the results of the preceding phase? *If not, consider how and why the results of the preceding phase were not approved. Ask yourself: "Should we really continue to the next phase without reworking the deliverables, changing the formal project specifications, or otherwise changing our project plans?"*

YES	NO	QUESTIONS
❏	❏	Has the authorization for this phase been issued by a manager external to the project and at a high enough organizational level to help meet project needs? *If not, identify an appropriate sponsoring manager and figure out how you can get his or her authorization.*
❏	❏	Is it clear who the project manager is for this phase? *If not, find out who should identify the project manager and what steps are needed to get the manager officially identified.*
❏	❏	Is the project manager authorized to apply organizational resources (people, equipment, materials) to the phase? *If the project manager has not been formally authorized, then ask the sponsor by whose authority project resources will be applied.*
❏	❏	Has the project manager been given the green light to continue with this project phase? *If not, decide what conditions need to be met to get authorization and begin to meet them.*

Remember: If the phase isn't authorized, you probably should not be expending resources (including your own time) working on it!

Action Tool: Describe Project Scope ☑

Assignment

Create an adequate description of project scope.

Desired Outputs

- Statement of project scope, which should include:

    - Project justification

    - List of major project deliverables

    - List of project objectives (quantifiable criteria that must be met for success. At minimum: cost, schedule, and quality measures.)[27]

- Scope management plan, which should include:

    - How the scope will be managed (i.e., how scope changes will be identified and integrated into the project)

    - Expected stability of the project[28]

- Work breakdown structure—a "family tree" that organizes and defines the total scope of the project.[29]

Checklist: Evaluating the Project Scope

Instructions: This checklist is designed to help you evaluate your description of the project scope.[30] Using the list below, check off the items that you have completed. (*If you are working with a formal or informal advisory group, you might ask all of its members to work through this checklist with you.*)

❏ There is a clear project justification (i.e., a clear explanation of why the project has been undertaken).

❏ There is a list of all major project deliverables.

❏ There is a list of project objectives.

❏ The project objective list includes quantifiable criteria for success, including:

- Cost criteria (i.e., What cost limits must be met in order for the project to be judged a success?)
- Schedule criteria (i.e., What calendar dates must be met in order for the project to be judged a success?)
- Quality measures (i.e., By what measures will we know that the project has produced quality deliverables or achieved quality results?)

❑ Project objectives do *not* take the form of fuzzy descriptions such as "to provide maximum customer satisfaction" or "to create state-of-the-art deliverables."

❑ There is a description of what constitutes an "out-of-bound" condition that might lead to a change in project scope (e.g., excess costs, schedule extensions, reduction in quality, increase in deliverables).

❑ There is a description of what to do when project scope changes are identified (e.g., notify sponsor, execute a contract change order, stop project work).

❑ There is a description of the expected stability of the project (e.g., "We have anticipated and spelled out potential unstable factors.")

❑ There is a work breakdown structure (WBS) or a "family tree" chart that organizes and defines the total scope of the project.

❑ All the items above have been organized into a single, comprehensive document (see Worksheet: Project Scope Statement).

Worksheet: Project Scope Statement

Project Name: _____ **Date:** _____

Project Manager: _____

Project Tracking No.:_____

Project Justification (Problem or Opportunity Addressed):

Overall Project Goal or Mission Statement:

Overview of Deliverables (broad brush only— place detailed work breakdown structure in appendices):

Specific Project Objectives and Success Criteria (schedule, cost, quality):

Scope Management Issues (including ways that scope changes will be handled, contract change orders will be processed, etc.):

Primary Stakeholders and Roles (including a broad statement of the roles and responsibilities of all customers, sponsors, contributors, reviewers, managers, sign-off authorities, project managers, etc.):

Key Assumptions:

Risks and/or Obstacles and Plans to Address These:

Signatures—The following people agree that the above information is accurate:

• Project team members:

• Project sponsor and/or authorizing manager(s):

---

*Appendices (Needs Analysis/Feasibility Study Notes, Detailed Work Breakdown Structure, Preliminary Schedule, Preliminary Cost Estimate, Sample Deliverables, Background Memos/Reports, Organization Chart of Project Team, others as needed).

Example: Work Breakdown Structure (WBS)

A *work breakdown structure* describes the components and subcomponents of the project's various work products as a "family tree." [31] Consider this example: A couple has decided that they would like to change their lifestyle by moving to their own custom-made log cabin in the wilderness. Below is a work breakdown structure for this project.

Note that the client shows *all* the various outputs that must be created, not just the most obvious. We can see, for example, that getting the financing arranged and the services installed will be important project outcomes, so the couple must account for these in their plans. Had they focused only on the most obvious (the cabin's construction), they might have overlooked these outcomes.

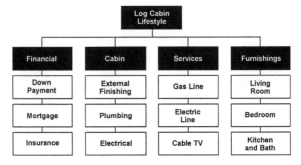

FIGURE 4. Work Breakdown Structure Chart

As this example shows, one of the main benefits of starting a project with a work breakdown structure is that it keeps the project manager focused on uncovering all the "hidden" deliverables. Only after all these specific outputs are examined in detail can the project manager develop an accurate list of activities (i.e., the project work tasks) necessary to create these deliverables.

Action Tool: Define and Sequence Project Activities

Assignment

Define and sequence all the activities necessary to complete the project.

Desired Outputs

- An activity list (list of all activities that will be performed on the project)

- Updates of the work breakdown structure (WBS) (*For details, see Action Tool: Describe Project Scope.*)

- A project network diagram showing the relationships among project activities

Guidelines for Defining and Sequencing Project Activities

Instructions: Follow these steps to define and sequence your project activities. You may use the check boxes to mark the items as completed. (*If you are working with a formal or informal advisory group, you might ask its members to work through these guidelines with you.*)

STEP 1: Assemble the following:

❑ Description of project scope

❑ Historical data and activities that were required for similar projects (i.e., What activities are usually completed for similar types of projects?)

❑ One or more experts who have defined and sequenced activities for similar projects

STEP 2: Create detailed activities lists.

❑ Examine the work breakdown structure, and for each product (deliverable) to be created, make a list of specific activities.

❑ Group these activities into clusters or groups of related activities. Keep in mind the typical project phases required by your industry's best practices.

❑ Separate some of the clustered activities into activities that can "stand alone."

❑ Identify review, revision, and sign-off points, if appropriate.

❑ Identify closure points for completing deliverables.

STEP 3: Create the project network diagram.

❑ Draw a diagram showing the relationships among activities (which one must come first, which must come next, which ones may proceed at the same time, etc.).

STEP 4: Evaluate the detailed list of activities and the network diagram, and revise/adjust.

❑ Revisit your network diagram and list of activities, and decide if they can be refined in any way.

❑ Ask an outside advisor (an expert in the project activities) to evaluate your network diagram and supporting activity list.

❑ Consider expanding or adding a level of detail to all activities whose measures of quality, cost, or schedule are unclear.

Example: Project Network Diagram

When you have listed all your project tasks and have figured out all of the task relationships, you are ready to organize them into a network diagram. [32] Such a diagram can highlight important relationships among project activities, allowing project planners to analyze these relationships and, if necessary, change them. Figure 5 shows two different types of network diagrams. Both of the diagrams below illustrate a do-it-yourself kitchen remodeling project. The kitchen owner has decided to repaint the walls, regrout the tile on the countertop, and install some new appliances. Note how the progress from one project activity to another can easily be seen in the diagrams.

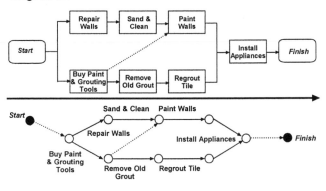

FIGURE 5. Network Diagrams for Kitchen Remodeling Project

Action Tool: Estimate Durations for Activities and Resources Required

Assignment

Estimate the duration of the activities and the resources that are required to complete those activities.

Desired Outputs

- Estimate of duration (time required) for each activity, and assumptions related to each estimate

- Statement of resource requirements (What people, equipment, and materials will be needed for each activity?)

- Updates of activity list (How will the activity list need to be modified, now that we have looked at duration and resources in greater detail?)

Guidelines for Estimating Durations for Activities and Resources Required

Instructions: Follow these steps to estimate the duration for project activities and the resources required. You may use the check boxes to mark items as completed. (*If you are working with a formal or informal advisory group, you might ask its members to work through this worksheet with you.*)

STEP 1: Assemble the following:

❑ Scope statement

❑ Activity list and network diagram

❑ Description of the resource pool, including resources available and their capabilities

❑ Historical data on similar activities from project files, commercial databases, or project team knowledge

❑ Organizational policy regarding staffing, rental/purchase of equipment and supplies, and so forth

❑ One or more experts who have estimated the duration and the required resources for similar projects

---

STEP 2: Examine each activity, and then estimate its duration and probable resources required (see Worksheet: Estimating Durations for Activities and Resources Required).

❏ Estimate of duration for each activity

❏ Estimate of resources required for each activity

❏ Assumptions about the resources to be assigned (for example, employees will need to work 10-hour days, or the machine will need to process 75 units per hour, etc.)

Note: Some organizations can supply you with data on what can reasonably be expected from a particular resource in order to achieve a quality work product. For example, a reasonable expectation for a veteran bricklayer might be to lay X number of bricks per day. If the project manager is forced to hire fewer bricklayers or inexperienced bricklayers due to budget cuts, then you may not be able to maintain your project schedule. Your assumptions should clearly state any "reasonable expectancies" such as these so that they are included in your project plan.

❑ Maximum time some staff members are able to devote to a particular activity

STEP 3: Re-evaluate the activity relationships, given your duration and resource assumptions.

❑ Examine clusters or groups of related activities.

❑ Examine "stand alone" activities.

STEP 4: Adjust the project network diagram as needed.

❑ Network diagram adjusted

STEP 5: Informally present your estimates of durations and resources required to an expert colleague as a reality check; then adjust it as needed.

❑ Expert review and adjustment completed

Worksheet: Estimating Durations for Activities and Resources Required

Instructions: In the *Activity* column, list the phases and activities that must be completed. In the *Duration* column, list the amount of time required to complete each activity. In the *Resources* column, enter the names of all resources that are required to complete each activity. Resources should include all people (including contractors), equipment, facilities, and materials. In addition, your assumptions about experience level, brand names of equipment, facility or equipment specifications, number of resources, and so on should be clearly spelled out, since failure to procure resources with the assumed characteristics will likely impact the time required to complete the activity.

Phase and Activity	Duration (hours or days)	Resources Required with Assumptions
Total Time Required:		

Phase and Activity	Duration (hours or days)	Resources Required with Assumptions
Total Time Required:		

Action Tool: Develop a Project Schedule

Assignment

Develop a project schedule.

Desired Outputs

- *Project schedule* (planned start and finish dates for each activity) in the form of Gantt charts, network diagrams, milestone charts, or text tables

- *Supporting details*, as required, to show resource usage over time, cash flow projections over time, order/delivery schedules, and other schedule-related information

- *Schedule management plan* describing how schedule changes will be handled

Guidelines for Developing the Project Schedule

Instructions: Follow these steps to develop a project schedule. You may use the check boxes to mark items as they are completed. (*If you are working with a formal or informal advisory group, you might ask its members to work through these guidelines with you.*)

STEP 1: Assemble the following:

❑ Your estimates of duration and needed resources

❑ Information about availability of resources—how much or how many will be available and when

❑ Organization calendars—these identify when work is allowed (when resources will be available, which days are holidays, which days are vacation days, and so on)

❑ Project constraints, including:

    ❑ Imposed dates based on stakeholder requirements, seasonal weather, etc.
    ❑ Key events or major milestone completion dates
    ❑ Unusual assumptions about resources or duration

❏ A blank calendar or other blank form on which to record the schedule

STEP 2: On the blank calendar, label any holidays or other dates when resources won't be available.

❏ Identify holidays, vacations, and the like.

STEP 3: Examine each activity and its duration, and plot the activity on the calendar. On a separate page labeled *"assumptions,"* record any assumptions about the activity, including assumptions about the resources to be assigned.

❏ Plot activities, duration.

❏ List assumptions about resources.

STEP 4: After the days are plotted on a standard calendar, create other types of schedule displays that will be useful (e.g., Gantt charts, network diagrams, milestone charts, text tables).

❏ Create specialized project-wide charts, schedules.

STEP 5: If your project's network diagram or Gantt chart shows many different activities happening at the same time, consider finding the *critical path* and attempting to shorten it in order to reduce the project's overall duration. (The critical path is the sequence of activities that takes the most time to complete.)[33]

Here are some ways you can shorten the critical path:

❑ *Reduce the duration* of some of the activities. (Simply allow less time for them.)

❑ *Add more resources* to some of the activities. (If you assign more people or equipment, you can often reduce the time required. Be careful, however, since this can increase the coordination time required.)

❑ *Allow more hours* in the workday. (Allow for overtime or add another shift.)

❑ *Allow more workdays* in the schedule. (Allow for weekend or holiday work.)

- ❑ *Change the relationships of activities.* (Instead of performing some tasks sequentially, one at a time, perform them at the same time, in parallel fashion.)

- ❑ *Use slack time more effectively.* (Find slack between activities or "downtime" for some resources, and advance the schedule or plan to complete pending activities during this time.)

- ❑ *Redefine one or more project phases.* (Check to see if some activities contained within a phase are causing the phase to be delayed needlessly; then consider moving these activities to the next phase.)

- ❑ *Redefine "done."* (Consider whether some deliverables, particularly interim deliverables such as blueprints, prototypes, or drafts, might be defined as "finished" in a less complete form.)

- ❑ *Reduce the amount of deliverables* that a particular activity produces. (It takes less time to do less work!)

- ❑ *Reduce the overall project scope.* (Eliminate some work products, processes, or deliverables.)

Caution: After you have determined which of the methods you would like to use to shorten the critical path, you should discuss them with your sponsors or stakeholders. Since many of these methods result in fundamental changes in project structure, you should discuss the positive and negative effects they might have on the project, and obtain sponsor/stakeholder approval.

STEP 6: Consider making customized activity schedules. They could be tailored for executive overview, for individual categories of resources (e.g., electricians, carpenters, landscapers), or for special project teams (workers in Argentina, England, or France, for example).

❏ Create or consider creating customized schedules.

STEP 7: Informally present your preliminary schedules to an expert colleague as a reality check; adjust it as needed.

❏ Solicit feedback from a peer or expert.

Example: Project Schedules

A *Gantt chart* is a graphic display of schedule-related information. In the typical Gantt chart, activities are listed down the left side of the chart, dates are shown across the top or bottom, and planned activity duration is shown as a horizontal bar, placed according to the dates. A Gantt chart is sometimes called a "bar chart." Because the Gantt bars are proportionally longer for project activities that take longer to complete, Gantt charts can effectively display relative differences in duration of activities.

Choose a Gantt chart when you want to show which activities will take longer than others. Note that project management software packages create high-quality Gantt charts quickly and easily. A sample of a Gantt chart is shown below.

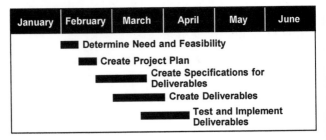

FIGURE 6. Sample of a Gantt Chart

A *network diagram*, as discussed in Action Tool: Define and Sequence Project Activities, shows which project activities depend on which other activities in order to be completed. Choose a network diagram when you want to clearly show the relationships among activities. Network diagrams may be presented with schedule data included on each activity description, as shown below. [34]

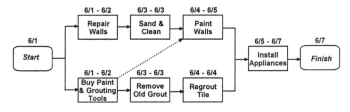

FIGURE 7. Network Diagram with Schedule Data

In addition, network diagrams may be time-scaled to show the relative amount of time passing between activities.[35] In the example below, we not only see the relative length of time to be spent on each activity, we have identified a delay or period of "downtime" between re-grouting the tile and installing the appliances.

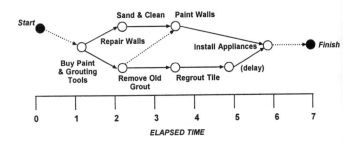

FIGURE 8. Network Diagram with Time Scale

Milestone charts show only the most significant project events. Choose a milestone chart when you want to provide broad overviews of the project's main events for executive audiences or others who want to see only the big picture.[36] Here is an example of a milestone chart:

Task Name	February	March	April	May	June
Feasibility Study Complete	3/1 ▲ Feasibility Study Complete				
Project Plan Complete	3/15 ▲ Project Plan Complete				
Blueprint Complete	4/1 ▲ Blueprint Complete				
Utilities Connected	4/15 ▲ Utilities Connected				
Cabin Frame Complete	5/1 ▲ Cabin Frame Complete				
Interior Finish Complete	5/15 ▲ Interior Finished				
Move In	6/3 ▲ Move In				

FIGURE 9. Sample of a Milestone Chart

In addition, project events and dates may be presented as *text tables*, as shown in Figure 10.

Date	Activity
Jan 15 - Mar 15	Conduct research
Mar 16 - Apr 16	Create detailed specifications for deliverables
Apr 16 - Apr 26	Sponsor review of detailed deliverable specifications

FIGURE 10. Sample of a Text Table

Finally, since everyone is familiar with its format, an *ordinary calendar* can be a powerful way to communicate the project schedule. As the example illustrates, a calendar can show relative duration and concurrence of activities, as well as days of the week and month, including weekends.

SUN	MON	TUE	WED	THUR	FRI	SAT
1 * Repair walls * Buy paint	2	3 * Sand, etc.	4 * Paint walls * Regrout tile	5	6 * Install appliances	7
8	9	10 * Shop around for new game room components ———————→	11	12	13	14
15	16 ←———————————	17	18	19 ————————→	20 * Design new game room	21
22	23	24	25	26	27	28
29	30	31				

FIGURE 11. Calendar Sample

You should select your schedule format carefully, keeping the needs of the audience in mind. Ask yourself:

- Who are the readers of this schedule?

- How much information do they need? ("Big picture" or details?)

- What form of schedule does this reader like (or expect) to see?

- Should I create customized versions of the schedule for certain audiences, certain activities or phases, or certain display purposes?

Action Tool: Estimate Costs

Assignment

Estimate the costs of completing all project activities.

Desired Outputs

- *Cost estimates* for completion of each activity

- *Supporting details*, including assumptions and constraints related to costs

- *Cost management plan* describing how cost variances will be handled

- *Revisions* to the project activity list or network diagrams in response to the need for more detail about costs

Example: A "Bottom Up"
Cost Estimate

There are three popular methods of cost estimating:

- *Bottom up estimating*—This means estimating the cost of individual activities and summarizing or "rolling up" these costs to determine project costs. (This method is preferred, since it is typically the most accurate, given unique project requirements.)

- *Analogous estimating*—Sometimes called "top down" estimating, this involves using the actual cost of a previous, similar project to make an estimate of costs for a planned project.

  Caution: Project managers should be sure to challenge the assumption that the previous analogous project was actually similar to the project they are planning. It must be truly similar in order for the cost estimates to be accurate.[37]

- *Fixed budget estimating*—taking the total amount of money you have available for the project and dividing it across the various project components to see what you can and can't afford.[38]

Figure 12 is an example of a "bottom up" cost estimate. In this sample, we have estimated the cost of removing brush from a vacant lot. This one-day project will involve one laborer, one truck driver/laborer, and one supervisor/laborer. In addition, we have assumed that we will need to rent a truck to carry the brush away, and pay a fee at the landfill to dispose of the brush.

Note that the worksheet lists all activities, the amount of time each activity will take, and the resources to be applied to complete each activity. Note also that some resources (the workers) will incur costs based on the number of hours they take to perform the task. These are typically referred to as *variable cost* resources, since the cost varies according to the effort expended.

Other resources (like the truck and landfill dumping fee) are typically referred to as *fixed cost* resources, since they involve a one-time cost, no matter how much effort is expended. Finally, note that the worksheet is designed to provide total costs for each resource, for each activity, and for the entire project.

Activity	Duration	Resource Name: Laborer Resource Rate: $10/hour — Cost of Resource for This Activity	Resource Name: Truck driver/laborer Resource Rate: $15/hour — Cost of Resource for This Activity	Resource Name: Supervisor/laborer Resource Rate: $20/hour — Cost of Resource for This Activity	Misc. Costs	Total Costs for Activity
Travel to site	1 hr.	$10.00	$15.00	$20.00	$150.00 rent truck	$195.00
Determine strategy for clean up	.5 hr.	$5.00	$7.50	$10.00		$22.50

FIGURE 12. Sample Cost-Estimation Worksheet— Brush Removal Project

Remove brush	3 hrs.	$30.00	$45.00	$60.00		$135.00
Load brush in truck	1 hr.	$10.00	$15.00	$20.00		$45.00
Haul brush to landfill	.5 hr.	$5.00	$7.50	$10.00		$22.50
Unload brush at landfill	1 hr.	$10.00	$15.00	$20.00	$25.00 dump fee	$70.00
Return from site	1 hr.	$10.00	$15.00	$20.00		$45.00
Return truck	.5 hr.			$10.00		$10.00
TOTAL:	8.5	$80.00	$120.00	$170.00	$175.00	$545.00

99

FIGURE 12. Sample Cost-Estimation Worksheet—Brush Removal Project (continued)

This example is overly simplified in order to illustrate the relationship among cost elements. However, when you plan your projects, you will likely need to add many more columns for resources and break down "Misc. Costs" into subcategories based on the deliverables you are creating. In addition, you should consider adding blanks for contingency fees, administrative costs, profit, and other items related to your particular organization's needs.

Guidelines for Making a
"Bottom Up" Cost Estimate

Instructions: Follow these steps to develop a project cost estimate using the "bottom up" estimating technique. You may use the check boxes to mark items as completed. (*If you are working with a formal or informal advisory group, you might ask some of its members to work through these guidelines with you.*)

STEP 1: Assemble the following:

❑ Descriptions of all project activities

❑ Description of resource requirements

❑ Description of resource rates (e.g., how much resources will cost per hour or per day)

❑ Duration estimates for each activity

❑ Historical data regarding costs of activities, resources, and projects

STEP 2: Set up a worksheet similar to the same worksheet shown earlier.

❑ Set up worksheet.

❑ Consider making a new spreadsheet using a template electronic spreadsheet file from a similar project or consider

---

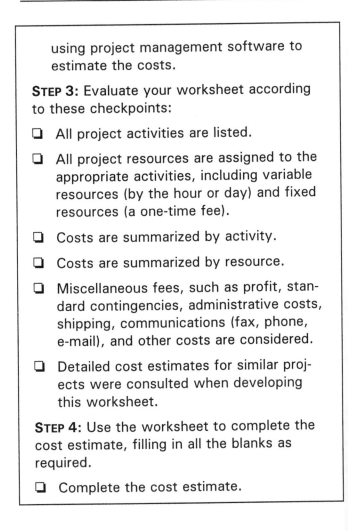

using project management software to estimate the costs.

STEP 3: Evaluate your worksheet according to these checkpoints:

☐ All project activities are listed.

☐ All project resources are assigned to the appropriate activities, including variable resources (by the hour or day) and fixed resources (a one-time fee).

☐ Costs are summarized by activity.

☐ Costs are summarized by resource.

☐ Miscellaneous fees, such as profit, standard contingencies, administrative costs, shipping, communications (fax, phone, e-mail), and other costs are considered.

☐ Detailed cost estimates for similar projects were consulted when developing this worksheet.

STEP 4: Use the worksheet to complete the cost estimate, filling in all the blanks as required.

☐ Complete the cost estimate.

STEP 5: Informally present your preliminary cost estimate to an expert colleague as a reality-check; adjust it as needed.

❏ Give it a reality-check.

STEP 6: Create summaries of costs and/or graphic displays of costs for presentation to stakeholders.

❏ Create cost summaries and graphics.

Action Tool: **Build a Budget and Spending Plan**

Assignment

Build a project budget and spending plan.

Desired Outputs

- A cost baseline or time-phased budget that will be used to measure and monitor project costs

- A spending plan, telling how much will be spent on what resources at what time

- A set of procedures which project team members will use to monitor costs and update the budget[39]

Guidelines for Building a
Budget and Spending Plan

Instructions: Follow these steps to create a budget and spending plan. You may use the check boxes to mark items as they are completed. (*If you are working with a formal or informal advisory group, you might ask some of its members to work through these guidelines with you.*)

STEP 1: ASSEMBLE THE FOLLOWING:

❑ Project cost estimates

❑ Work breakdown structure (WBS)

❑ Project schedule

❑ Budget forms or sample budget/spending plans approved by your organization

STEP 2: MAKE A WORKSHEET WITH HEADINGS SIMILAR TO THESE:

Activity	Account Code	Budgeted, January	Budgeted, February	Budgeted, March	Budgeted, April (etc.)

Note: If you want to monitor your spending on a quarterly or weekly basis, then label the column headings accordingly.

❑ Worksheet is completed.

STEP 3: List all project activities in the left column of the worksheet.

❑ Project activities are listed.

STEP 4: For each activity, examine the project schedule and cost estimate to determine how much will be spent the first month, how much the second month, and so on. Then list the appropriate dollar amounts in the columns beside each activity.

❑ Dollar amounts are listed by time.

> *Note: You might want to create a more detailed spending plan by breaking out specific resource costs under each activity. Consider the example provided on the following page.*

STEP 5: Informally present your preliminary budget and spending plan to an expert colleague for feedback; adjust as needed.

❑ Budget spending plan is given a reality-check and revised.

Activities/Resources	Account Code	Budgeted, Jan 1-7	Budgeted, Jan 8-15	Budgeted, Jan 16-23
Write Script				
• Scriptwriter	PRD-5	$2,000.00	$2,000.00	—
• Research Assistant	RAS-1	500.00	—	—
• Computer Rental	EQP-1	100.00	100.00	100.00
Review Script				
• Producer	PRD-1			$3,000.00
• Videographer	PRD-3			1,000.00
• Technical Reviewer	EXP-1			1,000.00
Total:		$2,600.00	$2,100.00	$5,100.00

STEP 6: Present your budget and spending plan to your supervisor and (if appropriate) to the sponsor; adjust as needed and obtain approval.

❑   Budget spending plan is approved.

Optional Action Tool: **Create a Formal Quality Plan** ☑️

Assignment

Create a quality plan.

Desired Outputs

❑ Quality management plan, including operational definitions

❑ Quality verification checklists

❑ Amendments to the project activity list, budget, and schedule to allow implementation of the quality plan

Guidelines for Creating a Formal Quality Plan

Instructions: Follow these steps to build a formal quality plan. You may use the check boxes to mark items as they are completed. (*If you are working with a formal or informal advisory group, you might ask some of its members to work through these guidelines with you.*)

STEP 1: Assemble the following documents:

❑ Your organization's quality policy

❑ Project scope statement

❑ Project product description (preliminary deliverables specifications)

❑ Standards and regulations

❑ Descriptions of process outputs in particular project team disciplines

STEP 2: Analyze each of the items assembled in Step 1, and distill from each item a list of operational definitions of quality.

❑ For each item, complete this statement: "According to this item, quality means..."

❑ Compile the items in a list and sort them into related groups.

STEP 3: Based on the list created in Step 2, make checklists that the various project team members can use to inspect for quality. (Checklists should be expressed as "Do this..." or "Have you done this...?")

❏ Checklists are created.

STEP 4: Develop a statement describing how quality management will be implemented on the project. It should describe specific methods of:

- **Quality control**—*examining specific project results to see if they comply with quality standards, and identifying ways to eliminate causes of unsatisfactory performance.*[40]

- **Quality assurance**—*evaluating overall project performance on a regular basis to instill confidence that the project will satisfy the relevant project quality standards.*[41]

❏ Statement of quality control and quality assurance is developed.

Optional Action Tool: Create a Formal Project Communications Plan

Assignment

Develop a project communications plan.[42]

Desired Output

A communications management plan that includes:

- Collection structure

- Distribution structure

- Description of information to be disseminated

- Schedules listing when information will be produced

- A method for updating the communications plan

Guidelines for Developing the Project Communications Plan

Instructions: Follow these steps to build your project communications plan. You may use the check boxes to mark items as they are completed. Refer to the Worksheet: Project Communications Planner, as needed. (*If you are working with a formal or informal advisory group, you might ask some of its members to work through these guidelines with you.*)

STEP 1: Assemble the following:

❑ List of project stakeholders and their roles, responsibilities, and physical locations

❑ Any descriptions of communication requirements or related assumptions among stakeholders

❑ Information about external reporting requirements (What do the public, the press, the government, and other outsiders need to know about the project? How will they find out?)

❑ Information about technology available to support communication on the project (e.g., fax, e-mail, voice mail, messenger, postal service, radio)

❑ Information about typical project communications methods for the industry or in your organization

STEP 2: Answer this question: "What kind of information does each stakeholder need?"

❑ List of information needed by each stakeholder

❑ Typical information needed by stakeholders on similar projects

STEP 3: Analyze all stakeholder information needs and answer this question: "What methods/technologies will provide all the information needed by stakeholders, without wasting resources by providing unneeded information or using inappropriate technology?"

❑ List of appropriate communications methods and technologies

STEP 4: Create a project communications plan that includes information about:

❑ Collection structure—How and by whom will project information be gathered, what information will be gathered, and from whom?

❑ Distribution structure—To whom will information flow, and by what methods?

❑ Description of each type of information to be disseminated—What format, content, level of detail, conventions/ definitions will be used?

❑ Schedules listing when each type of information will be produced

❑ A method for updating the communications plan as the project progresses

Worksheet: Project Communications Planner

Instructions: Look at the chart on the following page. In the **Who** column, list all the different project stakeholders who will be needing information as the project unfolds. (You may want to list some stakeholders as a group, such as "Engineering" or "Marketing." However, be careful that you have a clear idea about the specific people within the group to whom communications should be going.)

In the **What Information** column, list the type of information this person or group will need.

In the **When** column, list how often or at what points in the project this person or group will need the information. (For example, you might say "weekly" or "monthly" here, or "at sign-off of Phase II.")

In the **How (Form/Medium)** column, list the appropriate medium of communication. (For example, you might say "e-mail status report," "team meeting," "broadcast voice mail," or "update to project web page.")

Who?	What Information?	When?	How? (Form/Medium)

Action Tool: Organize and Acquire Staff

Caution: This Action Tool describes comprehensive organizational planning and staffing approaches, which might be "overkill" for a smaller project. Use your judgment to determine how many of the elements listed here make sense for your project.[43]

Assignment

Develop an organizational plan and a strategy for acquiring staff.

Desired Outputs

Desired outputs include:

- Role and responsibility assignments
- Staffing plan
- Organizational chart
- Organization detail, as appropriate
- Project staff
- Project team directory

Guidelines for Developing the Organizational Plan and Strategy for Acquiring Staff

Instructions: Follow these steps to develop the organizational plan and strategy for acquiring staff. You can use the check boxes to mark items as they are completed. (*If you are working with a formal or informal advisory group, you might ask some of its members to work through these guidelines with you.*)

STEP 1: Given your description of project activities in earlier statements, list the job titles (roles) of people who will be needed to complete each activity.

❑ Job titles or roles are listed.

STEP 2: For each job title, list the responsibilities (tasks) to be performed. Consult these sources as needed:

- Project templates—role and responsibility definitions from similar projects.

- Organization-specific human resource practices—policies, guidelines, and procedures that dictate how people are deployed (e.g., Will managers serve as "coaches?" If so, then what exactly is the role of "coach"?).

❑ Job responsibilities are listed.

STEP 3: Create a Responsibility/Account-
ability Matrix; refer to the example below.[44]

RESPONSIBILITY/ACCOUNTABILITY MATRIX					
Phase ↓ Person →	Bill	Alia	Juan	Leticia	Mary
Determine need and feasibility	A	S	P	P	P
Create project plan	A	S, I	I	I	I
Create specifications for deliverables	A, P	S	R	P	P
Create deliverables	A, R	S	P	P	P
Test and implement	A	I	R	R	P
P=Participate A=Accountable R=Review I=Input Required S=Sign-off Required					

❑ Responsibility/Accountability Matrix is
created.

STEP 4: Create a staffing plan that answers
these questions:

- When and how will people be added?

- Will the project use both internal and
  external resources? (Refer to Action
  Item: Plan for and Acquire Outside
  Resources)

- When will people be "let go" from the project team?

- How long should people be held when there is "downtime" (absence of work on their assigned activity)? [45]

❏ Staffing plan is created.

STEP 5: Create an organization chart that graphically displays project reporting relationships.[46] The chart should take into account reporting relationships among:

- Different organizational units (subcontractors, departments, etc.)

- Different technical disciplines (engineers, builders, etc.)

- Different individuals

❏ Organization chart is created.

STEP 6: Flesh out the organizational plan with these details as needed:

- Warnings describing what you will not be able to do if you cannot staff the project as recommended. (Describe what project deliverables cannot be created, how the schedule will be delayed, how safety might be jeopardized, and so on.)

- Specific job descriptions or position descriptions, including job title, skills, responsibilities, knowledge, authority, expected physical work environment, and so on.

- Training needs, if the staff to be hired or assigned does not have all the required skills.

❑ Warnings related to essential staffing are stated.

❑ Job descriptions and training needs are detailed.

STEP 7: Use appropriate procurement practices to identify and recruit resources. Take into account the staffing plan from Step 4, as well as standard recruiting practices dictated by your organization's policies (*also see "Optional Action Item: Plan for and Acquire Outside Resources."*)

❑ Identify resources.

❑ Recruit resources.

❑ Confirm resources as part of project team.

STEP 8: When all (or most) staff positions have been filled, create a project team directory consisting of:

- Names of team members and stakeholders

- How to reach each person listed (fax, phone, e-mail, postal service address, and so on)

- Other information such as direct reports, responsibilities, administrative support people, and so on as needed

❑ Project team directory is created.

Note: Will you be working with experts whose area of expertise is unknown to you? If so, review the Guidelines: Tips for Working with Experts Outside Your Area of Expertise.

Worksheet: Project Responsibility/ Accountability Matrix

Instructions: Using the matrix on the next two pages, list the project phases, activities, or deliverables in the first column. Label each of the remaining columns with the name of a project team member. Fill in the blanks underneath each team member's name with the appropriate initial to indicate his or her role related to this phase, activity, or deliverable. (Example: "I" for input, "S" for sign-off, etc.) Try to avoid using more than one initial per cell on the grid. *Note:* For best results, consider making this a team effort and complete the worksheet early in the project.

PROJECT RESPONSIBILITY/ACCOUNTABILITY MATRIX

Phase* ▶	Person ▶								

P = Participate A = Accountable R = Review I = Input Required S = Sign-off Required

*This column might also be labeled "activities" or "deliverables."

PROJECT RESPONSIBILITY/ACCOUNTABILITY MATRIX

Phase* ➤	Person ➤							

P = Participate A = Accountable R = Review I = Input Required S = Sign-off Required
*This column might also be labeled "activities" or "deliverables."

126

Guidelines: Tips for Working with Experts Outside Your Area of Expertise

Try some of these techniques for working with experts outside your area of expertise.

❑ Get them involved early on in the project, and ask them to help you plan, in detail, all the activities associated with their part of the project.

❑ Openly express your respect for their professional judgment, and frequently seek their opinions.

❑ Let them know that you aren't pretending to know their profession.

❑ Don't try to micromanage their specific actions. Instead, focus on their results by repeatedly referring to the deliverables specifications and formal statement of project scope.

❑ Ask them to provide you with overview information relating to their field. (These might take the form of handbooks, primers, slide presentations, promotional videos, and so on.)

❏ Ask them to describe for you the essential characteristics of finished products and work processes in their field. In other words, find out where their professional values lie and in what situations you can expect them to fight for these values.

❏ Single out a "friendly" expert and ask him or her to help you learn the jargon, acronyms, and underlying values of the profession. Ask this person to coach you or help you prepare for difficult meetings with his or her colleagues.

❏ Try to establish some basis of commonality. Go to lunch and get acquainted. Do you both enjoy hiking? the movies? your children? Remember, when you regard each other as people and not merely as robots performing job roles, you are both more likely to spend the energy necessary to achieve understanding.

Optional Action Tool: Identify Risks and Plan to Respond ☑

Assignment

Given a potential project, identify risks and plan to respond to them.

Desired Output

A document that describes the following:

- Sources of risk
- Potential risk events
- Risk symptoms
- Ways to improve other processes or activities
- Opportunities to pursue or threats to which to respond
- Opportunities or threats to ignore
- Risk management plan
- Contingency plans
- Descriptions of desired reserves
- Contractual agreements to mitigate risks.[47]

Guidelines for Identifying Risks and Planning to Respond

Instructions: Follow these steps to identify project risks and to plan responses to them. You may use the check boxes to mark items as they are completed. (*If you are working with a formal or informal advisory group, you might ask its members to work through these guidelines with you.*)

STEP 1: Determine what sources of risk and which risk events may reasonably be expected to affect the project.[48]

❑ Examine the product (deliverables) description. Which ones will have to be developed using unproven technology? Which deliverables are themselves made up of unproven technology?

❑ Examine the scope statement. Are the project costs or objectives overly aggressive?

❑ Examine the work breakdown structure. Is there anything "hidden" that should be explored? Can the work breakdown structure be broken into greater detail in some areas to shine a light on risks or opportunities? If so, then create this detail.

❑ Examine the staffing plan. Are there irreplaceable team members who might not be available at some point?

❑ Examine the resource requirements (people, equipment, and materials). Will a change in market conditions make it difficult to obtain some resources (a risk), or easier to obtain some resources (an opportunity)?

❑ Examine the history of similar projects. What potential opportunities or threats might we identify, based on previous experience?

❑ Use established checklists from your project's discipline to evaluate risk and opportunities.

❑ Interview various stakeholders to uncover opportunities or risks.

STEP 2: Quantify the risks identified in Step 1 to determine which risk events warrant response. Consider:

- Expected monetary value or impact of the risk
- Expected impact on project quality
- Expected impact on project schedule

❑ Risks are quantified.

STEP 3: Decide which risks or opportunities to focus on and document them by making a list of "risks to pursue."

❑ "Risks to Pursue" list is created.

STEP 4: For each risk warranting response, choose one of these risks responses:

- Avoid it—by eliminating the cause. This might involve using different approaches to the work process, different staffing, redefined deliverables, revised (lower-risk) schedules, or modified stakeholder expectations.

- Mitigate it—by reducing the expected monetary value. For example, you could:

  ❑ Contract out high-risk activities to specialists who have more experience.
  ❑ Obtain insurance policies to deal with some types of risk.
  ❑ Develop contingency plans that identify specific actions that will be taken if an identified risk should occur.
  ❑ Set aside a "desired reserve" of cash or other resources to use if the risk occurs.

- Accept it—and take the consequences.

(***Note:*** See the Worksheet: Risk Assessment and Response Analyzer.)[49]

❑ Each risk is examined and a decision to avoid, mitigate, or accept it is made.

STEP 5: Create a risk management plan that contains these sections:

- List of potential risk events

- Description of risk symptoms

- Ways to improve processes or activities to reduce risks

- Opportunities to pursue or threats that should be addressed

- Opportunities or threats that have been identified and consciously ignored

- Description of contingency plans and steps to take to mitigate risks

- Recommended contractual agreements to mitigate risks

❑ Risk management plan is created.

Worksheet: Risk Assessment and Response Analyzer

Instructions: Make a list of risks to your project. Using the grid on the following page, examine each risk separately and try to place it in the appropriate grid cell. Using the hints provided in each cell, determine an appropriate response to the risk.

For example, let's say that we are managing a technical project that faces the risk of losing the only scientist who understands the science behind the project. This would be enormously damaging to the project. At the same time, we know that she is being aggressively pursued by other companies and is unhappy with her current salary. This means it is highly likely that she will leave before the project is completed. Given these circumstances, this risk fits into the upper right grid square (high potential damage, high likelihood). So our overall approach should be to avoid this risk—eliminate its cause. We can do this by obtaining a higher salary for her, by hiring someone else with equivalent expertise as a back-up, or by insisting that she thoroughly train others so they develop her level of expertise.

(Avoid—Eliminate the cause)

(Mitigate—Create a Plan B, etc.)

(Mitigate—Create a Plan B, etc.)

(Accept)

Likelihood of Risk Occurring

Potential Damage to Project

Optional Action Tool: Plan for and Acquire Outside Resources

Assignment

Describe your strategy for procuring outside goods or services, soliciting bids, and selecting the best contractor for the job.

Desired Output

A procurement management plan indicating the following:

❑ Types of contracts to be used among contractors or vendors

❑ How estimates from vendors will be obtained

❑ Responsibilities of the project management team versus people in any "procurement" department

❑ How to use any standardized procurement documents

❑ Statement of work (SOW) or statement of requirements (SOR) describing the item (product or service) to be procured. The statement should provide prospective contractors with enough detail so that they can evaluate their ability to provide the item

❑ Bid documents, such as RFP (request for proposal), IFB (invitation for bid), invitation for quotation, and other similar documents

❑ Contract with one or more suppliers of goods or services.[50]

Guidelines for Planning to
Procure Outside Goods or Services

Instructions: Follow these steps to plan to procure (acquire) the help of outside contractors to provide certain goods or services for your project. You may use the check boxes to mark items as they are completed. (*If you are working with a formal or informal advisory group, you might ask some of its members to work through these guidelines with you.*)

STEP 1: Assemble the following:

❏ Statement of project scope

❏ Detailed product description (details of all deliverables to be created)

❏ Description of resources that support procurement (procurement department, internal project experts who can help find contractors, professional directories, and so on)

❏ Information on market conditions for the particular type of contractor you need

❏ Any relevant planning inputs, such as cost estimates and quality management plans

---

❑ Constraints and assumptions that will likely limit options (such as funds or schedule)

STEP 2: Decide to "make or buy" the goods or services.

❑ Examine the costs and benefits of creating the goods or services yourself. Consider:

- Workload of existing resources

- The time required to locate and acquire additional resources (such as new staff or new equipment)

- Your expertise in managing these resources

- Whether you want to have this resource available on an ongoing basis, as part of your organization

❑ Examine the costs and benefits of procuring the goods or services from an outside contractor. Consider:

- The actual cost of purchase compared to the cost of using internal resources

- The costs of having to solicit bids and select vendors (including "headaches" and time)

- The services external contractors can provide that your organization cannot or should not be able to provide on an ongoing basis

❑ Involve subject-matter experts from the project team, industry groups, consultant organizations, or even prospective contractors in these preliminary discussions.

❑ Decide to buy goods or services from an outside resource.

Note: If you decide to make the goods or perform the services internally, stop here.

STEP 3: Create a procurement management plan indicating the following:

- Types of contracts to be used among contractors or vendors

- How estimates from vendors will be obtained

- Responsibilities of the project management team versus responsibilities of people in any "procurement" department

- How to use any standardized procurement documents[51]

❑ Procurement management plan is created.

STEP 4: Create a statement of work (SOW) or statement of requirements (SOR) describing the item (product, deliverables, or service) to be procured. The statement should provide prospective contractors with enough detail so that they can evaluate their ability to provide the item.[52]

❑ Statement of Work or Requirements is created.

STEP 5: Create bid documents, such as RFP (request for proposal), IFB (invitation for bid), invitation for quotation, and similar documents.[53]

❑ Refer to any standard forms required by your organization.

❑ Refer to past versions of these documents for similar projects, and use "boilerplate" text if appropriate.

❑ Discuss your draft bid documents with someone who has solicited bids similar to yours.

❑ Finalize your RFP, IFP, or similar document.

STEP 6: Create bid/proposal evaluation criteria (means of scoring contractors' proposals). Consider these typical criteria and possibly weight some of them to count higher than others:

- Cost
- Quality
- Vendor team members
- Track record
- Facilities and equipment
- Creativity of proposal
- Referrals from former customers
- Ability to meet the schedule

❑ Bid/proposal evaluation criteria are established.

Guidelines for Soliciting Bids for Outside Goods or Services

Instructions: Follow these steps to solicit bids or proposals from outside contractors to provide certain goods or services for your project. You may use the check boxes to mark items as they are completed. (*If you are working with a formal or informal advisory group, you might ask some of its members to work through these guidelines with you.*)

STEP 1: Identify potential suppliers by asking for peer recommendations (people in professional groups, competitor organizations, others in your organization who know good potential vendors) or by examining listings of suppliers in directories of professional organizations, and so on.

❏ Potential suppliers are identified.

STEP 2: Decide whether to send out bid documents, advertise in professional journals or newspapers, or conduct a bidder's conference to solicit bids.

❏ Decide how to disseminate requests for bids.

STEP 3: Send out bid documents, conduct the bidder's information session, and/or place advertisements.

❑ Send out bid documents.

STEP 4: Clarify questions from potential contractors as needed.

❑ Clarify contractor questions.

STEP 5: Accept bids or proposals as they arrive, and disseminate them to fellow decision makers as appropriate.

❑ Accept, disseminate bids or proposals among decision makers.

Guidelines for Selecting the
Best Contractor for the Job

Instructions: Follow these steps to choose the best contractor from several who have submitted bids or proposals to provide certain goods or services for your project. You may use the check boxes to mark items as they are completed. (*If you are working with a formal or informal advisory group, you might ask some of its members to work through these guidelines with you.*)

STEP 1: Review your bid/proposal evaluation criteria (means of scoring contractors' proposals). (*See Step 6 of the Worksheet: "Guidelines for Planning to Procure Outside Goods or Services."*)

❑ Evaluation criteria are reviewed.

STEP 2: Set up a bid/proposal scoring sheet, which might include a weighting system (numerical weight assigned to each criterion) and a statement of minimum requirements (e.g., "Bid must be under $50,000 and maintain a schedule of no longer than 4 months").

An example of such a scoring sheet is provided on the following page.

Criteria	Possible Score	Jones Corp.	Smith Corp.	XYZ Corp.
Cost	6	4	6	6
Track Record	8	8	5	5
Team Members	10	10	10	5
Creativity	10	7	10	10
(. . . and so on)	...	...	...	...
Total Score	34	29	31	26

❑ Scoring sheet is created.

STEP 3: If appropriate, screen each bid or proposal and eliminate some on the basis of failing to meet the minimum requirements.

❑ Preliminary "cut" is completed; some contractors are eliminated.

STEP 4: Review all qualifying proposals and apply scoring criteria. If appropriate, ask a peer to cross-check your evaluations. (This person should be an experienced buyer of outside services who can help you cut through the "puffery" typically found in contractor proposals. It would be even more valuable if this person has direct experience working with one or more of the bidders.)

❑ Bids or proposals are scored.

STEP 5: Decide on the best vendor or contractor for the job.

❑ Contractor or vendor is selected.

STEP 6: Negotiate a contract with the vendor.

❑ Consider, if you have not already done so, the pros and cons of each of these types of contracts:

- Fixed price or lump sum contracts—A fixed total price is paid to the contractor for providing a clearly specified set of goods or services.

- Cost reimbursable contracts—The costs associated with providing the goods or services are reimbursed to the contractor. These are often used when goods or services to be provided are "fuzzy" or difficult to contain. They may include financial incentives for meeting or exceeding certain schedule or cost targets.

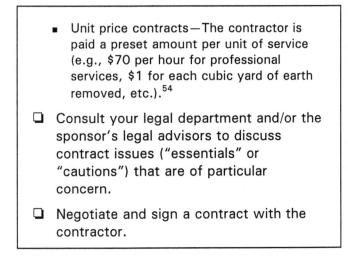

- Unit price contracts—The contractor is paid a preset amount per unit of service (e.g., $70 per hour for professional services, $1 for each cubic yard of earth removed, etc.).[54]

❑ Consult your legal department and/or the sponsor's legal advisors to discuss contract issues ("essentials" or "cautions") that are of particular concern.

❑ Negotiate and sign a contract with the contractor.

Action Tool: Organize the Project Plan ☑

Assignment

Create a comprehensive project plan.

Desired Output

A comprehensive project plan that pulls together all the outputs of the preceding project planning activities. (*See the guideline on the following page for a detailed description of the project plan components.*)

Guidelines for Creating the Project Plan

Instructions: Follow these steps to develop a formal, written plan for your project. You may use the check boxes to mark items as they are completed. (*If you are working with a formal or informal advisory group, you might ask some of its members to work through these guidelines with you.*)

STEP 1: Assemble all the outputs of the preceding action tools (i.e., scope statement, cost estimates, schedules, quality plan, etc.).

❑ Outputs of preceding planning Action Tools are assembled.

STEP 2: Develop an outline or table of contents for your project plan. It might include any of the following, as appropriate for your project:

■ Project charter—document issued by senior management that provides the project manager with the authority to apply organizational resources to project activities

■ Scope statement—description of the sum of the products and services to be provided by the project

---

- Work breakdown structure (WBS) to a level of detail that will be used to execute the project
- Cost estimates, scheduled start dates, and responsibility assignments to the level of the WBS at which control will be exercised
- Progress measurement baselines for time and cost
- Major milestones
- Key or required staff
- Key risks (including constraints and assumptions) and planned response for each
- Open issues and pending decisions
- Other information as needed for the particular project
- Appendices or supporting documents with detailed information such as technical documentation, preliminary specifications, preliminary designs, and so forth[55]

STEP 3: Review your outline with the sponsor and key stakeholders. Obtain their feedback regarding enhancements.

❑ Project plan outline is reviewed with stakeholders.

STEP 4: Revise your outline based on the results of Step 3.

❏ Outline is revised.

STEP 5: Write the project plan by connecting the pieces you assembled in Step 1.

❏ Write an overall introduction to the plan.

❏ Write transitions to help the reader comprehend the connections (inevitable linkages) among parts of the plan.

❏ Write an "Executive Summary" summarizing and highlighting the contents of the plan.

❏ Circulate a draft of the plan for review.

❏ Obtain feedback and revise and re-circulate as needed.

STEP 6: Circulate the final project plan among sponsor/customer and key stakeholders.

❏ Project plan is circulated among sponsor/customer and key stakeholders.

Action Tool: Close Out the Project ☑️
Planning Phase

Assignment

Close out the project planning phase.

Desired Outputs

- A project plan that has been approved by sponsor/customer and key stakeholders

- Documentation (written and signed documents) indicating that the sponsor:

  ❑ Approves the project plan

  ❑ Provides a "green light" or okay to begin work on the project

Guidelines for Closing Out the Project Planning Phase

Instructions: Follow these steps to plan to close out the project planning phase for your project. You may use the check boxes to mark items as they are completed. (*If you are working with a formal or informal advisory group, you might ask some of its members to work through these guidelines with you.*)

STEP 1: If you have not already done so, circulate the formal project plan among reviewers, including sponsor and key stakeholders.

❑ Project plan is circulated.

STEP 2: Conduct a formal, face-to-face meeting with the sponsor and key stakeholders in which you do the following:

❑ Briefly "walk through" the project plan, highlighting important sections for attendees.

❑ Discuss each of the sections until all attendees are comfortable with the plan.

Caution: Be certain to face up to the most controversial parts of the plan and discuss them at length. Do not avoid them or gloss

---

over them, since they may come back to haunt you later and you may need considerable sponsor support to overcome associated difficulties.

❏ Obtain concurrence among attendees about the plan, and if appropriate, decide on a strategy for modifying the plan.

❏ Present the sponsor with a "sign-off" document which indicates his or her approval of the entire project plan, with annotations listing needed changes. (See *Sample Project Sign-Off Form* in *Action Tool: Close Out Project Activities*.)

❏ Obtain the sponsor signature on the sign-off document.

Note: If you cannot obtain sponsor approval of the plan, decide which sections need to be modified and agree upon a strategy for making modifications and a deadline for completing them. Repeat Steps 1 and 2 if necessary.

STEP 3: After you have obtained formal approval of the project plan, summarize the results of the meeting and send out to other parts of the organization a formal announcement providing a thumbnail description of the project.

Caution: Do not begin the project without formal, public approval of the project plan from the sponsor. To do so will signal that you are taking responsibility for expending the organization's resources without authority or sponsor support.

Action Tool: Revisit the Project Plan and Re-plan If Needed ☑

Assignment

Review the approved project plan at the beginning of each project phase to make certain that the plan is still accurate.

Desired Output

Confidence on the part of the project manager that the detailed plans to execute a particular phase are still accurate and will effectively achieve results as planned.

Guidelines for Revisiting the Plan and Re-planning If Needed

Instructions: Follow these steps to confirm that the project plan remains accurate for a particular project phase. You may use the check boxes to mark items as they are completed.

STEP 1: Locate the detailed project plan, as approved at the end of Phase II: Create Project Plan.

❏ The detailed project plan is located.

STEP 2: Examine all project plans as they relate to this particular phase.

❏ All project plans are examined.

STEP 3: Evaluate the plans by considering these questions:

Yes	*No*	
❏	❏	Is the scope for this phase still accurate?
❏	❏	Is the project budget still accurate?
❏	❏	Is the project staffing plan still accurate?
❏	❏	Is the list of the project's sponsors and key stakeholders still accurate?

If "yes" to all of these questions, then continue to Step 4.

If "no" to any question, then immediately contact the sponsor or sponsors to decide whether it is necessary to repeat some or all of the action tools described in Phase II: Create Project Plan.

STEP 4: When you are satisfied that you have an accurate project plan, then you may begin this particular project phase.

❏ Plan is accurate. It's okay to begin this project phase.

Action Tool: Execute Project Activities ☑

Assignment

Execute a particular project activity or phase as planned.

Desired Outputs

- Work results (deliverables associated with this activity or phase) are created as a result of executing the project activities.[56]

- Change results (i.e., changes resulting in expanded or contracted project scope related to deliverables specifications) are identified.[57]

- Periodic progress reports summarizing results of activities are created.[58]

- Team performance is assessed, guided, and improved if needed through training and other interventions (e.g., team building, reward, and recognition).[59]

- Bids/proposals for deliverables associated with this phase are solicited, contractors (suppliers) are chosen, and contracts are established.[60]

- Contracts are administered to achieve desired work results (communication with contractors is undertaken to obtain work as planned, contract changes are prepared and negotiated as needed, contractors are paid).[61]

Guidelines for Executing a Project Phase

Instructions: Follow these steps to execute a particular project phase or activity. You may use the check boxes to mark items as completed.

STEP 1: Review the project plan carefully and get a clear picture of what the results of this phase should be.

❑ Project plan is reviewed.

STEP 2: If appropriate, conduct a kickoff meeting to get the phase off to a good start. The kickoff meeting should accomplish these objectives:

- Clarify work product (deliverables)

- Clarify roles and responsibilities of team members

- Create a shared sense of purpose among team members

- Obtain specific commitment of each team member to complete assigned activities according to schedule and budget constraints

- Make sure all team members have what is needed to begin work on this phase.

❑ Kickoff meeting is planned.

❑ Kickoff meeting is conducted.

Note: Small projects will likely have only one kickoff meeting, scheduled immediately after approval of the formal plan is obtained. Large, complex, or long-duration projects might require kickoff meetings at the beginning of each project phase.

STEP 3: Provide oral or written authorization to project team members to begin work on their activities at the appropriate times, as needed.

❑ Team members are authorized to begin.

STEP 4: Set up and conduct status review meetings and/or routine status reporting procedures.

❑ Status reporting procedures are established.

❑ Status reports are obtained.

Caution: Make sure meetings are truly justified and waste no team member's time. Consider conference calls or other "non-travel" options for geographically distant team members.

STEP 5: Based on team performance, provide training and other interventions (team building, reward and recognition, etc.).

❑ Necessary team training, rewards, and recognition are identified.

❑ Team training, rewards, and recognition are provided.

STEP 6: Circulate reports of progress according to the project's communications plan. Report progress of deliverables in terms of schedule, cost, and quality considerations.

❑ Progress reports are circulated.

Repeat Steps 3 through 6 as needed.

Note: The following checklist, *Keeping Things Moving*, and other corresponding tools may help you execute your project phases. Review these and apply them as appropriate to your project.

Action Tool: Control Project Activities ☑

Assignment

Take steps to control the project's activities.

Desired Outputs

- Decision to accept inspected deliverables

- Corrective actions

- Rework of deliverables

- Adjustments to work process

- Updates to project plan and scope

- Revised deliverables estimates

- Revised cost estimates

- Updates to risk management plan

- Updates to activity list or work breakdown structure

- List of lessons learned

- Improved quality

- Completed evaluation checklists (if applicable)

KEEPING THINGS MOVING:
A "To Do" List and Tools to Help You Execute, Control, and Close Out Your Project

Instructions: After your project plan is approved and you are up and running, you can use the checklist below and the attached tools to help you keep things moving according to your plan.

Go through this list at least weekly for each project you are managing.

❑ CHECK YOUR PROJECT'S SCOPE.

Refresh your memory about your project's goals and boundaries. In particular, make sure you have a clear picture of what the desired results should be at this point relative to deliverables, schedule costs, quality, and so on. (*See Worksheet: Project Scope Statement under Action Tool: Describe Project Scope if you don't already have a formal scope statement.*)

❑ CHECK YOUR DELIVERABLES.

Analyze the status of each project deliverable. Are they evolving as planned? If appropriate:

1. Locate *lists of quality criteria* that may be applied to inspect the quality and completeness of the deliverables at this stage of the project.
2. Check *contractors' proposals or contracts* to make sure you know what they should be supplying at this point.
3. Inspect all project deliverables.

4. Decide whether to accept inspected deliverables or to require rework.

(*See Worksheet: Project Deliverables Status Analyzer.*)

❑ **CHECK YOUR SCHEDULE.**

Examine your milestones, key dates, and critical path. Are you where you need to be?

❑ **ANALYZE VARIANCES (DEVIATIONS FROM PLAN) BY COMPARING "ESTIMATED" TO "ACTUAL."**

1. Are activities taking longer than planned? (Are you exceeding estimates of duration?)
2. Are you using more resource hours than you planned?
3. Are your actual costs exceeding your estimated costs?
4. If minor variances are discovered (variances that can be resolved easily without changing the plan or scope), then resolve them.
5. If major variances are discovered (variances that change the scope or constitute significant project issues), then handle them as described in the steps below.

(*See Worksheet: Variance Analyzer.*)

❑ **ADDRESS SCOPE CHANGES.**

1. Identify changes in scope (changes in deliverables, schedule, costs, etc.).
2. Handle scope changes, if necessary.

(*See Guidelines: Handling Scope Change* and *Worksheet: Project Scope Change Order.*)

❑ **LIST, TRACK, AND TRY TO RESOLVE OPEN ISSUES.**
  1. Make a list of all the unresolved issues, or
  2. Revisit the list of open issues from the last inspection period and try to resolve them.
  (*See Worksheet: Project Issue Tracker.*)

❑ **REVISIT POTENTIAL PROJECT RISKS.**
  1. Locate the Risk Management Plan, if one has been created.
  2. Note particularly whether any of the ongoing events or upcoming events are identified in the risk management plan as particularly vulnerable to risk.

❑ **REPORT PROJECT STATUS.**
  1. After completing the checks above, if you haven't already done so, talk to your team members and determine their perspective on project status.
  2. Create and circulate a project status report.
  (*See Worksheet: The Project Status Report.*)

❑ **DRIVE FOR CLOSE-OUT OF ACTIVITIES AND SIGN-OFF OF DELIVERABLES AS APPROPRIATE.**
  1. Ask yourself, "What activities can I close out? Which deliverables can I get formally approved and signed-off?"
  2. Prepare and get signatures on sign-off forms as appropriate.
  (*See Worksheet: Sample Project Sign-off Form* under *Action Tool: Close Out Project Activities.*)

❑ **DECIDE WHETHER IT'S NECESSARY TO KILL THE PROJECT, THEN DO SO IF APPROPRIATE.** (See Appendix B: Guidelines—When to Kill the Project.)

❑ **CREATE A LIST OF LESSONS LEARNED.**
Create a list of lessons learned that describes the ways subsequent project activities must be modified in order to prevent the difficulties encountered up to this point.

❑ **COMPLETE APPROPRIATE EVALUATION CHECKLISTS.**
Complete evaluation checklists, if applicable, and file them as part of the official project records.

Worksheet: Project Deliverables Status Analyzer

Deliverable:			As of:		
	Work Product (Deliverable) Status	Quality Level	Schedule Status	Team Status	Cost Status
Ideal State:					
Current State:					
Issues/Obstacles/ Risks:					

Continued . . .

170

Ways to Remove Issues/Obstacles/Risks					
To Do: *What:*					
Who:					
Deadline:					
To Do: *What:*					
Who:					
Deadline:					

171

Concluded

WORKSHEET: VARIANCE ANALYZER

Instructions: This worksheet will help you analyze variances (deviations from plan) by comparing "estimated" to "actual." ***Enter*** the name of a project phase ("Phase:") and then list all related project activities. ***Next,*** examine your project plan. ***Then,*** for each activity, list the estimated duration, total labor hours, and costs (Est. Dur., Est. Hrs. and Est. $$) allocated for completing that activity. ***Next,*** enter the actual time elapsed (Act. Dur.), actual labor hours consumed (Act. Hrs.), and actual costs (Act. $$) related to completing each activity. ***Finally,*** compare all actuals (Act. . .) with estimates (Est . . .) to determine all the variances from plan (Var. . .).

For example, if you estimated an activity to be 10 days and it only required 8 days, then you have a positive variance of 2 days for the duration of the activity. Alternately, if you estimated that an activity might consume 80 labor hours and it actually required 100 labor hours, then you have a negative variance of 20 hours for the activity's labor hours. As these examples illustrate, you should subtract *Actual* from *Estimated* to determine *Variance.* To complete the analysis, note any explanations for the cause of the variance.

Continued . . .

Phase:	Est. Dur.	Act. Dur.	Var. Dur.	Est. Hrs.	Act. Hrs.	Var. Hrs.	Est. $$	Act. $$	Var. $$	Explanation
Activities:										

Continued . . .

173

Phase:	Est. Dur.	Act. Dur.	Var. Dur.	Est. Hrs.	Act. Hrs.	Var. Hrs.	Est. $$	Act. $$	Var. $$	Explanation
Activities:										

Concluded

Guidelines: Handling Scope Change

Background: Scope change may be defined as any addition, reduction, or modification to the deliverables or work process as outlined in your original project plan. Change of scope is normal — it's not necessarily a problem. In fact, scope changes can be beneficial when they allow the project team to respond sensibly to changing conditions that exist outside the project. This can help ensure that project deliverables remain relevant.

Project managers should approach changes of scope in a business-like (as opposed to emotional) fashion. The steps below outline a systematic process for dealing with scope change.

1. *Stay calm.* Remind yourself that the original project scope documents were created at a time when you knew less than you know now. Given the new knowledge and circumstances, you need to modify your plan. This will likely result in your having to ask for more time, more resources, more money, and other concessions from your sponsors or stakeholders. Realize that you'll simply need to analyze the situation and make a solid case for your new requirements. So there's no need to panic.

2. **Pinpoint the exact change.** Clearly and dispassionately state the exact scope of the change that is required.

3. **Analyze the impact of the change.** Specify how the change will impact:

   - Schedule
   - Quality of the finished product
   - Costs
   - Project team assignments, including level of effort
   - Other deliverables, including amount and quality

4. **Discuss the impact with your project team.** Assemble relevant team members and brainstorm alternatives for handling the change with as little impact as possible.

5. **Report the impact to the sponsor.** Make sure the sponsor is aware of implications of the change by discussing the change with the sponsor and his key stakeholder-recommenders.

6. **Update the project scope statement and overall plan.** Make an addendum or a complete revision, if appropriate, of the project schedule, work breakdown structure, scope description, and so on. Make sure you note all of the conditions

that led to the change, the people who discussed alternatives, and the people who selected the recommended alternative. Document it—get it in writing.

7. ***Obtain written sponsor approval*** of the change and the corresponding revised plan. To guard against "amnesia" on the part of the sponsor, make sure the sponsor signs a document acknowledging the scope change and its rationale.

Worksheet: Project Scope Change Order

Project Name: _____ **Date:** _____

Project Manager: _____

Project Tracking No.: _____ **Change No.:** _____

Summary of Change:

Rationale for Change:

Brief overview of the impact of this change on . . .

- Project schedule:

- Quality of deliverables:

- Costs:

- Stakeholders and/or core team members:

- Other deliverables, including amount and quality:

Change approved by (signatures):

Sponsor: _____ **Date:**_____

Project Manager: _____ **Date:** _____

Other: _____**Date:** _____

Worksheet: Project Issue Tracker

Project: _____ **As of:** _____

Description of Issue or Required Action	Date Named		Deadline to Resolve	Date Closed	Internal Team Member Resp.	External Team Member Resp.	Immediate To-Do Items, Comments, or How Resolved

Continued . . .

Description of Issue or Required Action	Date Named	Status (open or closed)	Deadline to Resolve	Date Closed	Internal Team Member Resp.	External Team Member Resp.	Immediate To-Do Items, Comments, or How Resolved

Concluded

Worksheet: The Project Status Report

Title: Project XXX Status Report
Date:
Author:

Accomplishments Since Last Report:

(Deliverables completed, milestones attained, decisions made, issues resolved, etc.)

-
-
-
-
-
-
-

Upcoming Activities:

(What the team must focus on accomplishing throughout the next reporting period.)

-
-
-
-
-
-
-

Summary of Issues, Concerns, and Recommended Actions:

(What issues or concerns are unresolved? Include recommended actions for each.)

•

•

•

•

•

•

•

Comments:

(Miscellaneous comments, public praise for extra effort, announcements, etc.)

•

•

•

•

•

•

•

Action Tool: Close Out Project Activities ☑

Assignment

Complete the close-out of a particular phase or activity.

Desired Outputs

- Formal acceptance, documented in writing, that the sponsor has accepted the product of this phase or activity (may be conditional)

- Formal acceptance of contractor work products (deliverables) and updates to the contractor's files

- Updated project records prepared for archiving (can include updates to historical databases extending beyond the project to the overall program)

- A plan for follow-up and/or hand-off of project work products

Guidelines for Closing Out
a Project or Phase

Instructions: Follow these steps to close out (bring to an "official" conclusion) a particular project phase or activity. You may use the check boxes to mark items as they are completed.

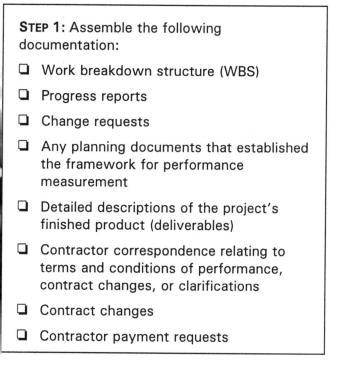

STEP 1: Assemble the following documentation:

❑ Work breakdown structure (WBS)

❑ Progress reports

❑ Change requests

❑ Any planning documents that established the framework for performance measurement

❑ Detailed descriptions of the project's finished product (deliverables)

❑ Contractor correspondence relating to terms and conditions of performance, contract changes, or clarifications

❑ Contract changes

❑ Contractor payment requests

STEP 2: Inspect to determine completion of the phase.

❑ Measure, examine, and test the work product (deliverables) to make certain that results conform to requirements. This might include conducting "walk-through" examinations, audits, reviews, and so on.[62]

❑ Conduct a procurement audit to identify contractor successes and failures.[63]

STEP 3: Conduct a project team review of successes, failures, lessons learned, methods or technologies developed that should be applied to other projects, and follow-up activities.[64]

❑ Team review is conducted.

STEP 4: Obtain formal evidence, documented in writing, that the sponsor has accepted the product of this phase. (This can be conditional, such as "Accepted with the understanding that XYZ deliverable will be reworked within 10 days at no cost.")

❑ Formal written acceptance ("sign-off") of project deliverables is obtained.

STEP 5: Declare formal acceptance of contractor work products (deliverables), and update the contractor's files.[65]

❏ Formal written acceptance ("sign-off") of contractor deliverables is completed.

❏ Contractor files are updated.

STEP 6: Update project records and prepare them for archiving. (This can include updates to historical databases extending beyond the project to the overall program.)[66]

❏ Project records are updated for archiving.

STEP 7: Plan to "hand off" or turn over work products to users by preparing written descriptions of how to use the work products, creating implementation guidelines, conducting training and support sessions, and so on.

❏ Plan for hand-off is developed.

STEP 8: Consider appropriate follow-up activities such as scheduled inspections of sponsors' use of the work product following implementation, follow-up analysis of product effectiveness, and so on. If appropriate, assign responsibility for the planned follow-up activities.

❑ Consider follow-up activities.

❑ Create follow-up plan.

❑ Assign follow-up activities to a specific person.

Worksheet: Sample Project Sign-Off Form

Project Name: XYZ System Upgrade

I have reviewed the following deliverables as of the date identified below:

•

•

•

•

•

I have found these deliverables to meet with my approval, with the following exceptions:

•

•

•

I hereby give my approval to proceed with the evolution of these deliverables to the next stage of development in order to meet the project objectives in a timely fashion.

I understand that any changes (additions, deletions, or modifications) to the fundamental structure, underlying design, or specific features of these deliverables might result in:

- Slippage of the completion date for these deliverables

- Additional resource requirements

- Additional costs

_____ *[Signature]*

J. Edgar Sponsor, V.P.
Systems Fluctuations

Date: _____

Appendices

Appendix A: Potential Shortcuts for
Low-Risk Projects

Appendix B: Guidelines—When to
Kill the Project

Appendix C: Glossary of Project
Management Terms

Potential Shortcuts for
Low-Risk Projects

In Part II we presented our **Summary of Key Project Manager Actions and Results**—a set of specific actions that project managers should take to help ensure the success of their projects. These actions provide certain checks and balances that are essential—especially if the project is complicated, controversial, highly visible, or managed by an inexperienced team. However, there are certain circumstances when fewer safeguards may be needed. For example, if you are the project manager *and* the sponsor, it might not be necessary to build in sponsor approvals in your project plans. If you are managing a relatively small project that employs time-tested processes that have become a matter of routine for your project team and that will lead to the deliverables whose need and feasibility are assured, you might be able to skip and/or abbreviate several of the key Project Manager Actions.

The table below shows how you can eliminate or abbreviate some of these Actions under certain circumstances. Here's what the symbols mean:

- This symbol ● means that the Action should be fully completed.

- This symbol ○ means that the Action can be abbreviated.

- This symbol — means that you can probably skip the Action altogether.

Action	Low-Risk Ex. 1: - The project is needed and is feasible - You are your own project sponsor	Low-Risk Ex. 2: - The project is needed and is feasible - The project is small and routine - The project employs time-tested activities
Initiating		
1. Demonstrate project need and feasibility	—	—
2. Obtain project authorization	—	○
3. Obtain authorization for the phase	—	○
Planning		
4. Describe project scope	○	○
5. Define and sequence project activities	●	○

6.	Estimate durations for activities and resources required	●	○
7.	Develop a project schedule	●	●
8.	Estimate costs	●	●
9.	Build budget and spending plan	●	●
10.	(*Optional*): Create formal quality plan	—	—
11.	(*Optional*): Create formal project communications plan	—	—
12.	Organize and acquire staff	○	○
13.	(*Optional*): Identify risks and plan to respond	—	—
14.	(*Optional*): Plan for and acquire outside resources	—	—
15.	Organize the project plan	○	●

16. Close out the Project Planning Phase	—	●
17. Revisit the project plan and re-plan if needed	●	●
Executing		
18. Execute project activities	●	●
Controlling		
19. Control project activities	●	●
Closing		
20. Close out project activities	○	●

Guidelines—When to Kill the Project

A project often develops enormous momentum as team members devote large amounts of time and energy and even make substantial personal sacrifices (overtime, changes in personal plans, etc.) on behalf of the project. Yet there are some circumstances in which it simply doesn't make sense to continue—in other words, there are times when a project should either be abandoned completely or stopped, reviewed, and then completely replanned from scratch.

Here are some of the circumstances under which it might make sense to abandon the project:

❏ *When it no longer has strategic value.*
   When the project is no longer contributing to the organization's long- or short-term business strategies, no matter how wonderful the project's end product or process, it should probably be abandoned. Why consume resources for a non-strategic set of deliverables?

   Many project managers would say that this is the single most painful situation they face. It's tough to let go—especially when you're building a good product on time and within budget and you've invested a lot of yourself in the project. On the other hand, in today's lightning-fast business world, top managers must frequently abandon business strategies that aren't working or are no longer competitive—and this means directing subordinates to let go of projects that no longer make good business sense.

❑ **When it is simply no longer feasible.** When the project cannot be done properly with the available resources or under the current circumstances, it may make sense to abandon it.

❑ **When deliverables repeatedly fail to appear, despite the best efforts of the team.** If at first (and second, and third, and fourth!) you don't succeed, you should probably abandon your plan and start from scratch before wasting more resources.

❑ **When the deliverables are substantially and continually behind schedule.** In this circumstance, you should first try to adjust the scope, apply more resources, or adjust the quality level. If these fail, then the plan is likely bad and should be abandoned.

❑ **When there are more issues than successes.** Call them problems, concerns, or plain old troubles, but when issues outnumber the successfully completed milestones and deliverables, you probably have a poorly-designed project. The project should probably be abandoned and stakeholders (especially the issue-defining stakeholders) reassembled to design a new project from scratch—one that accommodates the issues.

❏ ***When budget or resource allocations are continually exceeded.*** This probably means a poor project design, including inadequate scope description, poor estimate of resources, and inadequate cost estimate. Consider rethinking the entire project and starting again with a more reasonable budget or resource allocation. If these can't be obtained, then reduce the deliverables, either in quality or quantity, so that they more realistically match the available resources and funds.

Glossary of Project Management Terms

Activity: A unit of work performed to complete a project. An activity typically takes time (duration) and expends resources. Activities are often broken down into a series of individual, but related, tasks.

Actual Cost of Work Performed (ACWP): The total costs that were incurred (direct and indirect) in accomplishing work during a given time period.

Actual Finish Date: The date that work actually stopped.

Actual Start Date: The date that work was actually begun on a particular activity.

Baseline: A fixed project schedule that represents the original plan for the project (including approved changes). The baseline is a yardstick against which the actual project plan is measured to detect deviations. Baselines can take the form of cost baselines, time or schedule baselines, and so on.

Budgeted Cost of Work Performed (BCWP):
The sum total of all approved cost estimates
for project activities completed during a
particular time period.

Budgeted Cost of Work Scheduled (BCWS):
The sum total of all approved cost estimates
for project activities that are planned or
scheduled to be performed during a particular
time period.

Calendar: A project calendar lists time intervals
in which activities or resources can or cannot
be scheduled. A project usually has one default
calendar for the normal work week (Monday
through Friday), but may have other calendars
as well. Each calendar can be customized with
its own holidays and extra work days.

Calendar Unit: The smallest unit of time used in
creating the project schedule (typically hours,
days, or weeks).

Chart of Accounts: A numbering system used
to label or categorize project costs. Typically,
the project's chart of accounts is consistent
with the overall organization's chart of
accounts.

Closing or Closing Out: Obtaining formal approval of the outputs of an activity, a phase, or the project as a whole. Typically project records are updated and deliverables are handed off.

Code of Accounts: A numbering system used to identify each component of the project's work breakdown structure.

Contingency Planning: The process by which a management plan is created to address certain potential project risks.

Control: The process of comparing actual performance with planned performance, analyzing the differences, and taking the appropriate corrective action. In addition, controlling involves updating the scope and plan as they change.

Critical Activity: Any activity that is on the project's critical path. A critical activity has zero or negative float. It must be finished on time or the whole project will fall behind schedule. (Non-critical activities have float or slack time and are not on the critical path. Super-critical activities have negative float.)

Critical Path: In the project's network diagram, the critical path is that path (or linked set of activities) that takes the most time to complete. All activities on the critical path must be completed on time; a delay in any activity on the critical path causes a delay in the completion of the project. There may be more than one critical path, depending on duration and the way work flow is organized.

Critical Path Method (CPM): A method of determining project duration by analyzing the network diagram, finding the critical path, and making certain schedule calculations. CPM typically calculates the start and finish dates in two passes. The first pass calculates early start-and-finish dates from the earliest start date forward. The second pass calculates the late start-and-finish activities from the latest finish date backwards. The difference between the pairs of start-and-finish dates for each task is the float or slack time for the task. An advantage of this method is the fine-tuning that can be done to accelerate the project. After the initial calculation, the project manager can shorten various critical path activities, then check the schedule to see how it is affected by the changes. By experimenting in this manner, the optimal project schedule can be determined. (Project management software can greatly simplify CPM analysis by automating the forward and backward calculations and then graphically depicting the critical path. In fact, on larger projects, such calculations would be almost impossible if done manually.)

Deliverable: Any measurable, tangible, verifiable output that must be produced to complete the project. Deliverables take two forms: Interim outputs (such as video scripts, floor plans, or marketing analysis) and final deliverables associated with these interim outputs (such as the completed video presentation, the finished building, or a completed product marketing plan).

Duration Compression: Shortening the project's overall schedule by assigning more resources to perform some activities.

Earned Value: A method for quantifying and analyzing project performance by comparing the amount of work that was planned with what was actually accomplished. This allows the analyst to determine if cost and schedule are progressing as planned.

Earned Value: A method for quantifying and analyzing project performance by comparing the amount of work that was planned with what was actually accomplished. This allows the analyst to determine if cost and schedule are progressing as planned.

Early Finish: The earliest calculated date on which an activity can end. It is based on the activity's Early Start which depends on the finish of predecessor activities and the activity's duration. Most PM software calculates early dates with a forward pass from the beginning of the project to the end.

Early Start: The earliest calculated date on which an activity can begin. It is dependent on when all predecessor activities finish. Most PM software calculates early dates with a forward pass from the beginning of the project to the end.

Effort (or Work): The amount of labor required to complete an activity. Effort is usually expressed as person-hours or person-days.

Elapsed Time: The total number of calendar days (excluding non-work days such as weekends or holidays) that is needed to complete an activity.

Exception Report: A project report that shows only major deviations from the original plan (rather than all deviations).

Executing: Performing the activities of a project as planned; creating work results, making progress reports, and initiating change requests.

Fast Tracking: The process by which the project schedule is compressed by doing some or all activities in parallel instead of in linear sequence.

Finish Date: The calendar date at which an activity is to be completed.

Finish Float: The amount of excess time an activity has at its finish before a successor activity must start. This is the difference between the start date of the predecessor and the finish date of the current activity, using the early or late schedule. (Early and Late dates are not mixed.) This may be referred to as "slack time." All floats are calculated when a project has its schedule computed.

Finish-to-Start Lag: The minimum amount of time that must pass between the finish of one activity and the start of its successor(s). The finish-to-start lag is zero. If the predecessor's finish is delayed, the successor activity's start will have to be delayed. In most cases, finish-to-start lags are not used with other lag types.

Finish-to-Finish Lag: The minimum amount of time that must pass between the finish of one activity and the finish of its successor(s). If the predecessor's finish is delayed, the successor activity may have to be slowed or halted to allow the specified time period to pass. Finish-to-finish lags are often used with start-to-start lags.

Finishing Activity: The last activity that must be completed before a project can be considered finished. This activity is not a predecessor to any other activity—it has no successors.

Float: Sometimes called "downtime," "slack time," or "path float," float is the amount of time that an activity may be delayed from its start without delaying the entire project.

Free Float: The excess time available before the start of the following activity, assuming that both activities start on their early start date.

Functional Manager: A manager who is responsible for activities in a particular department or organizational function, such as accounting, advertising, manufacturing, and so on.

Functional Organization: An organization structure in which staff members are grouped hierarchically by their expertise or area of specialization, such as accounting, advertising, manufacturing, and so on.

Gantt (Bar) Chart: A graphic display of activity durations. Activities are listed with other tabular information on the left side, with time intervals over the bars. Activity durations are shown in the form of horizontal bars, which are proportionally longer or shorter, depicting relative differences in days', weeks', or months' duration.

Goal: A broad result toward which the project team directs its efforts, but which is less quantifiable and measurable than is a specific deliverable. For example, one project goal may be to increase the opportunities for shopping in a particular neighborhood. A related deliverable would be the creation of a 25,000-square-foot retail shopping space.

Hammock: A hammock groups activities, milestones, or other hammocks together for reporting.

Histogram: A graphic display of resource usage over a period of time. Usually created by project management software, histograms allow the user to see overused or underused resources. In PM software, the resource usage is displayed in colored vertical bars. The ideal level for a resource on the screen is indicated by another color (typically red). The vertical height is produced by the value specified in the maximum usage field of the Resource Label window. (The printed histogram uses a horizontal line to display the maximum usage set in the Resource Label window.) If the resource bar extends beyond the red area for any given day, resources need to be leveled (or spread out) for a more balanced allocation. The resource histograms should be checked after resources are assigned to the project activities.

Initiating: The process by which a project or project phase or activity is begun. Typically, initiating involves demonstrating project need and feasibility and obtaining authorization to begin.

Lag: The time delay between the start or finish of an activity and the start or finish of its successor(s).

Late Start: In the critical path method, late start dates are defined as the latest dates by which an activity can start to avoid causing delays in the project. Many PM software packages calculate late dates with a backward pass from the end of the project to the beginning.

Late Finish: In the critical path method, late finish dates are defined as the latest dates by which an activity can finish to avoid causing delays in the project. Many PM software packages calculate late dates with a backward pass from the end of the project to the beginning.

Lead: An overlap between activities in that the start of a task precedes the finish of its predecessor.

Master Schedule: A summary schedule that identifies all major activities and key milestones.

Matrix Organization: Any organizational structure in which project managers share responsibility with the functional managers for directing the work of people assigned to the project.

Micro-Scheduling: The scheduling of activities with durations of less than one day (in hours or fractional days).

Milestone: A significant event in the project, usually completion of a major deliverable. Milestones differ from project to project depending on the type of deliverables the project is designed to create. In project management software, a milestone is an activity that has been assigned zero duration (usually marking the end of an activity or phase).

Monte Carlo Analysis: A mathematical assessment method that performs a simulation of the project several times in order to calculate a distribution of potential results.

Multi-Project Analysis: Used to analyze the impact and interaction of activities and resources whose progress affects the progress of a group of projects. In particular, multi-project analysis is important when individual projects are sharing resources (people or equipment), since such analysis can help prevent overbooking. Multi-project analysis can also be used for composite reporting on projects having no dependencies or resources in common.

Near-Critical Activity: An activity that has very little total float.

Negative Float: Indicates activities must start before their predecessors finish in order to meet a target finish date. Negative float occurs when the difference between the late dates and the early dates (start or finish) of an activity is negative. In this situation, the late dates are earlier than the early dates. This can happen when constraints (activity target dates or a project target finish date) are imposed on a project.

Network Analysis: The process of identifying early and late start-and-finish dates for project activities. This is done with a forward and backward pass through the project. Many PM software tools will check for loops in the network and issue an error message if one is found. The error message will identify the loop and all activities within it.

Network Path: A path is a series of connected activities displayed in a network diagram.

Network Diagram: A network diagram is a graphic representation of the sequence and relationship of project activities. Activity boxes (nodes) are connected by one-way arrows to indicate precedence. The first activity is placed on the left side of the diagram, with the last activity on the right side. Activity boxes are usually placed at different levels (not in a single row) to accommodate activities that are done simultaneously.

Ongoing Operations: Those activities under-taken by an organization to routinely and repetitively generate the goods or services it has been set up to generate. Ongoing opera-tions are distinct from projects, which are temporary, finite, and unique.

Parallel Activities: Two or more activities that can be done at the same time. This allows a project to be completed faster than if the activities were arranged serially or in a linear sequence.

Phase: A collection of logically related project activities, usually resulting in the completion of a major deliverable. By organizing project activities into a few major phases, it is easier to plan the project, discuss project events with team members, and analyze and track the project. The exact phases used in a project typically are established by professional standards in a particular industry.

Positive Float: The amount of time that an activity's start can be delayed without affecting the project completion date. An activity with positive float is not on the critical path and is called a non-critical activity. Most software packages calculate float time during schedule analysis. The difference between early and late dates (start or finish) determines the amount of float. Float time is shown at the end or the beginning of non-critical activities when a bar chart reflects both early and late schedules.

Precedence Notation: A means of describing project work flow. It is sometimes called "activity-on-node notation." Each activity is assigned a unique identifier. Work flow direction is indicated by showing each of the activity's predecessors and their lag relationships. Graphically, precedence networks are represented by using descriptive boxes and connecting arrows to denote the flow of work.

Predecessor: An activity that must be completed (or be partially completed) before a specified activity can begin is called a predecessor. The combination of all predecessors' and successors' relationships among the project activities forms a network. This network can be analyzed to determine the critical path and other project scheduling implications.

Program: A group of related projects whose outputs are typically integrated or coordinated and whose activities are managed together. Programs often include an element of an organization's ongoing activities.

Program Evaluation and Review Technique (PERT): An event-oriented network analysis technique based on the use of a network diagram that shows dependencies between project tasks. In a PERT chart, activities are represented by boxes, or nodes, and relationships among activities are represented by lines that connect these nodes. In PERT analysis, each activity is assigned a best, worst, and most probable completion time estimate. These estimates are used to determine the average completion time. The average times are used to figure the critical path and the standard deviation of completion times for the entire project.

Project: A temporary endeavor undertaken to create a unique product or service. Typically, a project is a one-time effort to accomplish an explicit objective by a specific time. Like the individual activities that make up the project, each project has a distinguishable start and finish and a time frame for completion. Each activity in the project will be monitored and controlled to determine its impact on other activities and projects. Unlike an organization's ongoing operations, a project must eventually come to a conclusion. The project is the largest discrete block of time and resources handled by most PM software.

Project Charter: A document created and/or approved by upper management or the project sponsor that provides the project manager with the authority necessary to use organizational resources to complete project activities.

Project Life Cycle: A collection of project phases whose name and number are determined by the control needs of the organization or organizations involved in the project. For example, the project life cycle of a motion picture project would include such phases as casting, scripting, shooting, editing, and so on. In contrast, the project life cycle for a home building project might include such phases as creating the blueprint, building the foundation, framing the walls, and so on. In each case, the project phases are unique to the industry and designed to achieve specific project deliverables. Also in each case, the project phases allow the project deliverables to evolve gradually and systematically. In this way, the project manager and the professionals involved on the team can inspect the deliverables as they are emerging in order to control the quality, timing, and cost. By using an industry-standard project life cycle, project managers can help assure that deliverables will conform to recognized quality standards.

Project Management (PM): The application of knowledge, skills, tools, and techniques to project activities in order to meet or exceed stakeholder needs and expectations.

Project Management Professional (PMP): An individual certified as such by the Project Management Institute.

Project Management Software: A computer application specifically designed to help plan and control project costs and schedules.

Project Plan: A formal, approved document used to guide the execution and control of a project. The plan documents planning assumptions and decisions, and aids communication among stakeholders. In addition, the plan "puts in writing" the sponsor-approved scope, cost, and schedule baselines.

Project Planning: Developing and updating the project plan. This involves describing project scope, defining and sequencing project activities, estimating durations of activities and resources required to complete them, and developing the schedule. In addition, planning involves estimating costs, building a budget, organizing and acquiring staff, organizing and "selling" the plan, and obtaining approval of the plan.

Project Schedule: The planned calendar dates for completing activities and achieving milestones.

Project Team Members: The people who report to the project manager or work with him or her indirectly to accomplish project goals and complete project activities.

Projectized Organization: Any organizational structure in which project managers have all needed authority to assign priorities and to direct the work of people assigned to their projects.

Resource: A resource is anything that is needed to complete an activity. This may include people, equipment, materials, facilities, and so on.

Resource-Based Duration: In project management software, a method of calculation that provides the option to determine activity duration, remaining duration, and percent completed through resource usage. The resource requiring the greatest time to complete the specified amount of work on the activity will determine the duration of the activity.

Resource Leveling: The process of adjusting project schedules in order to minimize the peaks in daily resource usages. This is usually done when one or more resources are over-allocated (assigned to work more hours in a day than they can work). In resource leveling, activities are moved within their available float to produce a new schedule. In project management software, resources and projects may be assigned leveling priorities. Some activities may not have any rescheduling flexibility due to lack of float. PM software substantially simplifies this process, particularly when leveling on larger projects.

Schedule Variance: The difference between the scheduled completion date of an activity and the actual completion date of that activity.

Scheduled Start Date: The date work was scheduled to begin on an activity. The scheduled start date typically falls between the early start date and the late start date.

Scheduled Finish Date: The date work was scheduled to end on an activity. The scheduled finish date typically falls between the early finish date and the late finish date.

Scheduling: The process of determining when project activities will take place depending on defined durations and precedent activities. Schedule constraints specify when an activity should start or end based on duration, predecessors, external predecessor relationships, resource availability, or target dates.

Scope: The sum of the products (deliverables) and services to be provided as a project. The statement of project scope (a formal document) should include a list of deliverables, a list of project objectives, and a description of project success criteria, such as cost, quality, and schedule measures.

Scope Change: Any change made to the project scope. A scope change almost always leads to a revision of the project cost estimate and/or schedule.

Sequence: The order in which activities will occur relative to each another. This establishes the priority and dependencies between activities. Successor and predecessor relationships are typically developed and displayed in a network format. This allows those involved in the project to visualize the work flow.

Slack: The amount of time a task can be delayed without delaying the project completion date.

Slippage: The amount of slack or float time used up by an activity due to a delayed start. If an activity without float is delayed, the entire project will slip.

Stakeholders: Individuals and organizations who are involved in, or may be affected by, project activities. Typical stakeholders include the project sponsor (the person or organization paying the bills and able to stop the project— sometimes called client, customer, or funder), suppliers, contractors, vendors, craftspeople, the project manager, government agencies, and the public.

Start-to-Start Lag: The minimum amount of time that must pass between the start of one activity and the start of its successor(s).

Start Float: The amount of excess time an activity has between its early start and late start dates.

Starting Activity: An activity with no predecessors. It does not have to wait for any other activity to start.

Statement of Work: A narrative description of all products or services to be provided by a contractor.

Sub-Critical Activity: An activity that has a float threshold value assigned to it by the project manager. When the activity reaches its float threshold, it is identified as being critical.

Since this type of criticality is artificial, it normally does not have an impact on the project's end date.

Subnet or Subnetwork: The subdivision of a project network diagram into smaller components, each of which represents some form of subproject.

Subproject: A distinct group of activities that compose their own project, which in turn is a part of a larger project. Subprojects are sometimes summarized into a single activity to hide the detail and allow the activities to be viewed in summary form.

Successor: A successor is an activity whose start or finish depends on the start or finish of a predecessor activity.

Super-Critical Activity: An activity that is behind schedule. It has been delayed to a point where its float is calculated to be a negative value. The negative float is representative of the number of schedule units by which an activity is behind schedule.

Target Finish—Activity: An imposed finish date for an activity. A target finish date typically represents predefined commitment dates. Most

PM software will not schedule a late finish date later than the target finish date.

Target Finish—Project: An imposed completion date for a project as a whole. A target finish date is used if there is a predefined completion date. Most PM software will not schedule any late finish date later than the target finish date.

Target Start—Activity: An imposed starting date for an activity. Most PM software will not schedule an early start date earlier than the target start date.

Task: A subdivision of an activity; each activity may consist of several smaller tasks.

Time-Scaled Network Diagram: A project network diagram created so that the position of each activity represents its planned start date and finish date. In other words, it displays the relative durations of activities (like a Gantt Chart) but includes the lines and nodes of a network diagram.

Total Float: The excess time available for an activity to be expanded or delayed without affecting the rest of the project—assuming it begins at its earliest time. It is calculated using

the following formula: Total Float = Latest
Finish - Earliest Start - Duration.

Work Breakdown Structure (WBS): A
deliverables-oriented "family tree" of project
components (products or services) that shows
the total scope of the project. Each descending
level represents an increasingly detailed
definition of a project component. WBS is a
methodology that leads to definitions of the
hierarchical breakdown of responsibilities and
work in a project. Once implemented, the WBS
facilitates summary reporting at a variety of
levels.

Work Flow: The relationship of the activities in
a project from start to finish. Work flow takes
into consideration all types of activity
relationships.

Work Load: The amount of work units assigned
to a resource over a period of time.

Work Units: A measurement of effort
expended by resources. For example, people as
a resource can be measured by the number of
hours they work.

Work Package: The smallest unit shown in a work breakdown structure chart.

Zero Float: A condition where there is no excess time between activities. An activity with zero float is considered a critical activity. If the duration of any critical activity is increased (the activity slips), the project finish date will slip.

References

1. The Project Management Institute. *A Guide to the Project Management Body of Knowledge (PMBOK).* Copyright 1994 by the Project Management Institute, 130 South State Road, Upper Darby, PA 19082, page 2.

2. Ibid, pp. 6, 62

3. Ibid, p. 64

4. Ibid, pp. 6-7, 63

5. Ibid, pp. 7-8, 64

6. Ibid, pp. 6-8, 20

7. Ibid, pp. 6-8, 13-14

8. Ibid, pp. 6-8

9. Ibid, Ibid.

10. Ibid

11. Ibid, p. 13

12. Ibid, p. 12

13. Ibid

14. Ibid

15. Ibid, p. 13

16. Ibid, pp. 12-13

17. Ibid, p. 13

18. Ibid, pp. 13-14

19. Ibid, pp. 14-15

20. Ibid, p. 15

21. Ibid, pp. 15, 61

22. Ibid, p. 15

23. Ibid, p. 16

24. Ibid, p. 21

25. Ibid

26. Ibid

27. Ibid

28. Ibid

29. Ibid, pp. 22, 64

30. Ibid, p. 21

31. Ibid, p. 22

32. Ibid, p. 25

33. Ibid, p. 27

34. Ibid, p. 28

35. Ibid, p. 29

36. Ibid

37. Ibid, p. 31

38. Ibid, p. 43
39. Ibid, pp. 39-40
40. Ibid, p. 39
41. Ibid
42. Ibid, p. 40
43. Ibid, pp. 46-48
44. Ibid, p. 46
45. Ibid, p. 47
46. Ibid, pp. 51-53
47. Ibid, p. 51
48. Ibid, pp. 51-52
49. Ibid, p. 52
50. Ibid, p. 53
51. Ibid, pp. 18, 63
52. Ibid, pp. 17-19
53. Ibid
54. Ibid, pp. 43-44
55. Ibid, pp. 40-41
56. Ibid, pp. 52-53
57. Ibid, pp. 53-54
58. Ibid, p. 23

59. Ibid, p. 54

60. Ibid, p. 44

61. Ibid, p. 54

62. Ibid, p. 44

Subject Index

Action tools, identifying, 45–49. *See also individual project processes*

Activities
 for creating deliverables, 16, 17
 for creating a project plan, 13–14
 for determining need and feasibility, 13
 duration of, 78–83
 for testing and implementing deliverables, 18

Activity, defined, C-1

Activity list, 39, 74, 75, 78

Activity schedule, customized, 89

Activity-on-node notation, C-15

Actual cost of work performed, C-1

Actual finish date, C-1

Actual start date, C-1

ACWP. *See* Actual cost of work performed

Administrative closure, 33

Analogous estimating, 96

Analysis
 Monte Carlo, C-12
 multi-project, C-12–C-13
 network, C-13

Application specialists
 determining need and feasibility, 12
 specifications and, 14

Archiving, 184, 187

Audits, 186

Authorization, 38
    action tool, 58–62
    for budget, 108
    for close-out, 153, 155
    for phase, action tool, 63–66
    for project, 28, A-2
    for project activities, 163

Bar charts, C-9. *See also* Gantt charts
Baseline, defined, C-1
BCWP. *See* Budgeted cost of work performed
BCWS. *See* Budgeted cost of work scheduled
Benefits, 56. *See also* Cost-benefit analysis
    of deliverables, 37
    of procuring outside goods/services, 139
Bid documents. *See* Invitation for bid; Request
  for proposal
Bids
    selection guidelines, 142, 145–148
    soliciting, 31, 42, 136–137, 160
        guidelines, 143–144
Blueprints, 6, 9, 22
Bottom up cost estimates, 96–100
    guidelines, 101–103
Budgeted cost of work performed, C-2
Budgeted cost of work scheduled, C-2
Budgets, 29, A-3
    authorization of, 108
    creating, 40
        action tool, 104–108

exceeding, B-3
review of, 158

Calendar, C-2
    scheduling, 85–86, (illus.) 93–94
Calendar unit, defined, C-2
Cash flow projections, 40, 84
Change requests, 185
Change results, 160
Chart of accounts, C-2
Checklist, project scope, 68–69
Closing, 33–34, 42, A-3
    action tool, 153–156, 184–190
    activities, 168
    choosing action tools for, 46–49, 53
    defined, C-3
    results of successful performance, 44
    shortcuts, A-4
Closing out, C-3
Coaching, 31
Code of accounts, C-3
Communications plan, 29, 164, A-3
    action tool, 112–117
    creating, 41
Communications technology, 113
Concept definition, 13, 20
Constraints, 85
    in procuring outside goods/services, 139
Contingency planning, C-3

Contractors, 31
    correspondence with, 185
    payment requests, 185
    procurement audit and, 186
    selecting, 136, 145–148
Contracts, 136–137, 160–161, 166
    administration, 31, 42, 43
    changes, 185
    close-out, 33
    mitigating risk and, 129
    negotiation, 147–148
Control, defined, C-3
Controlling, 31–32
    choosing action tools for, 46–49, 53
    results of successful performance, 44
    shortcuts, A-4
Cost baseline, 40
Cost control, 32
Cost criteria, 68
Cost estimates, 29, 40, 105, 138, 151, A-3
    action tool, 95–103
    bottom up examples, 96–100
    updating, 165
Cost management plan, 40, 95
Cost monitoring, 104
Cost reimbursable contracts, 147
Cost-benefit analysis, 13, 20
Costs, 56
    of deliverables, 37
    of procuring outside goods/services, 139

CPM. *See* Critical path method
Critical activity, defined, C-3
Critical path, 87–89
    defined, C-4
Critical path method, C-4–C-5
Customized activity schedule, 89

Deliverables, 3, 6–7
    checking status of, 166
    creating, 14, 16–17, 23, 43, 48
    defined, C-5
    determining need and feasibility, 37
    failure of, B-2
    project life cycle and, 10
    project phases and, 8
    rework of, 165
    risk and, 130
    sign-off on, 168, 186–187, 189–190
    specifications for, 14–16, 22
    status analyzer, 170–171
    testing and implementing, 17–18, 24, 186
Delivery schedules, 84
Design plan, 22
Discretionary planning, 29–30
Documentation
    authorization, 153, 155
    close-out, 184, 186–187
    project scope change, 177
Downtime, C-8
Duration compression, C-5

Early finish, defined, C-6
Early start, defined, C-6
Earned value, defined, C-6
Effort, defined, C-6
Elapsed time, defined, C-6
Essential planning, 28–29
Estimates, vendor, 136. *See also* Bids
Evaluation checklists, 165, 169
Exception report, defined, C-7
Executing, 30–31
    choosing action tools for, 46, 48–49, 53
    defined, C-7
    results of successful performance, 43
    shortcuts, A-4
Experts, subject-matter, 140
    working with, 127–128

Fast tracking, defined, C-7
Feasibility, determining, 8, 12–13, 37, A-2, B-2
    action tools, 46, 54–58
    worksheet, 20
Feasibility study, as deliverable, 7
Finish date,
    defined, C-7
    schedule, C-21
Finish float, defined, C-7
Finished deliverables, 6–7
Finishing activity, defined, C-8
Finish-to-finish lag, defined, C-8

Finish-to-start lag, defined, C-7–C-8
Fixed budget estimating, 96
Fixed cost resources, 97
Fixed price contracts, 147
Float
    defined, C-8
    negative, C-13, C-24
    positive, C-15
    start, C-23
    total, C-25–C-26
    zero, C-27
Float time, C-22
Flowcharts, 9, 22
Follow-up, 184, 187–188
Free float, defined, C-8
Functional manager, defined, C-9
Functional organization, defined, C-9

Gantt charts, 40, 84, (illus.) 90, C-9
Goal definition, 13, 20
Goals, 54, 55. *See also* Objectives
    defined, C-9
Guidelines
    bid solicitation, 143–144
    bottom up cost estimates, 101–103
    budget and spending plan creation,
      105–108
    communications plan, 113–115
    contractor selection, 145–148

    duration of activities and resources
      estimate, 79–81
    organizational plan and staff acquisition
      development, 119–123
    outside goods/services procurement,
      138–142
    planning phase closing, 154–156
    project activity sequencing, 75–76
    project closing, 185–188
    project phase execution, 162–164
    project plan, 150–152
    project plan review, 158–159
    project schedule development, 85–89
    project scope change, 175–177
    quality plan creation, 110–111
    risk identification, 130–133
    when to discontinue project, 169, B-1–B-3
    working with experts, 127–128

Hammock, defined, C-10
Histogram, C-10
Human resources practices, 119

IFB. *See* Invitation for bid
Implementation, 9, 17–18, 24
    action tools, 49
Informal distribution, 31
In-house vendors, vs. outside, 139

Initiating, 28
    choosing action tools for, 46–49, 52
    defined, C-10
    results of successful performance, 37–38
    shortcuts, A-2
Interim deliverables, 6
Invitation for bid, 42, 137, 141

Job descriptions, 122
Job responsibilities, 119
Job titles, 119

Kickoff meeting, 162–163

Lag, defined, C-11
Late finish, defined, C-11
Late start, defined, C-11
Lead, defined, C-11
Lessons learned, 169
Leveling, resource, C-20–C-21
Life cycle. *See* Project life cycle
Lump sum contracts, 147

Managers, authorization and, 66
Market analysis, 8, 13, 20, 56
    as deliverable, 7
Market conditions, procuring goods/services
  and, 138
Master schedule, defined, C-11
Matrix organization, defined, C-12

Meeting, kickoff, 162–163
Micro-scheduling, defined, C-12
Milestone, defined, C-12
Milestone charts, 40, 84, (illus.) 92
Mitigation, of risk, 132, 135–136
Monte Carlo analysis, defined, C-12
Multi-project analysis, defined, C-12–C-13

Near-critical activity, defined, C-13
Need, determining, 8, 12–13, 37, A-2
    action tools, 46, 54–58
    worksheet, 20
Needs analysis, 13, 20
Negative float, C-24
    defined, C-13
Network analysis, C-13
Network diagram, 40, 81, 84, (illus.) 91–92
    defined, C-14
Network path, defined, C-14

Objectives, 67, 68, 70. *See also* Goals
Ongoing operations, defined, C-14
Order schedules, 84
Organization
    functional, C-9
    matrix, C-12
    projectized, C-20
Organization calendars, 85
Organizational chart, 41
    creating, 121–122

Organizational commitment, 28
Organizational plan, A-3
    action tool, 118–129
Outputs, 150
Outside resources, 42, A-3
    action tool, 136–148
Outside vendors, vs. in-house, 139
Overall change control, 32

Parallel activities, defined, C-14
Path float, C-8
Performance, actual vs. planned, 31–32
PERT. See Program Evaluation and Review
  Technique, C-16–C-17
Phase, defined, C-14–C-15
Planning, 28–30
    action tools, 153–156
    choosing action tools for, 46–49, 52–53
    document, 14
    project phases and (illus.), 34–36
    results of successful performance, 39–43
    shortcuts, A-2–A-4
PM. See Project management
PMBOK. *See* Project Management Body of
  Knowledge
PMP. See Project management professional
Positive float, defined, C-15
Precedence notation, defined, C-15
Predecessor, defined, C-16
Presentation, 57

Process, defined, 26
Procurement audit, 186
Procurement management plans, 29, 42, 136,
   140
Program, defined, C-16
Program Evaluation and Review Technique,
   defined, C-16–C-17
Progress measurement baselines, 151
Progress reports, 32, 43, 160, 164, 168, 185
Project, defined, 6, C-17
Project actions, 3–4
      determining, 36–45
Project activities, 25
      authorization of, 163
      close-out, 44, 168
         action tool, 184–190
      control, action tool, 165–184
      estimating duration of, 39
      execution,
      action tool, 160–164
      sequencing, 39, A-2
         action tool, 74–77
Project authorization, 28, A-2
Project charter, 38, 58, 60, 150
      defined, C-17
      worksheet, 61–62
Project concept, 8
      approval of, 13
Project constraints, 85
Project description, 56

Project issue tracker, 180–181
Project issues, B-2–B-3
Project justification, 67, 68
Project life cycle, 3, 6, 9–11, 35–36
    creating deliverables, 16–17
    creating project plan, 13–14
    creating specifications for deliverables,
      14–16
    defined, 9, C-17–C-18
    deliverables and, 10
    determining need and feasibility, 12–13
    generic (illus.), 11–12
    testing and implementation, 17–18
    worksheet, 19–24
Project management, defined, C-18
Project Management Body of Knowledge, 25
Project Management Institute, 1, 25
Project management processes (illus.), 25–27.
  See also Closing; Controlling; Executing;
  Initiating; Project management professional,
  defined, C-18
Project management software, C-18
Project manager
    assigning, 38
    determining need and feasibility, 12
    identifying, 58, 60, 66
Project network diagram, 74, 76
    example (illus.), 77

Project phases, 3, 6
    action tool, 63–66
    authorization for, 38
    deliverables and, 8
    identifying, 45–49
    project management processes and (illus.),
        34–36
Project plan, 8–9, 21, 29, 42, A-3, A-4
    action tool, 149–153
    choosing action tools for, 47
    creating, 8, 13–14
    defined, 8, C-19
    as deliverable, 7
    execution, 30–31
    review, 154, 162
        action tool, 157–159
    updating, 165
Project planning, defined, C-19
Project processes, identifying, 45–49
Project proposal, 57
Project schedule, 105, B-2
    action tool, 84–94
    criteria, 68
    defined, C-19
    developing, 29, 40, A-3
    management plan, 84
    reviewing, 167
Project scope, 39, 75, A-2
    action tool, 67–73
    checklist, 68–69

defining, 29
management plan, 67
procuring outside goods/services and, 138
review, 158
updating, 165, 166
verification, 33
Project scope change, 32, 167
defined, 175
guidelines for, 175–177
Project scope change order, 178–179
Project scope statement, 150
quality plan and, 110
risk and, 130
worksheet, 70–71
Project specifications
creating, 9
as deliverables, 7
Project status report, 182–183
Project strategy, 56
Project team directory, 123
Project team members, defined, C-19
Project team review, 186
Project templates, 119
Projectized organization, defined, C-20
Proposals. *See also* Bids
criteria, 142, 145
soliciting, 31, 160

Prototypes, 17, 23
    creating, 9
        as deliverables, 7
Providers, 31

Quality assurance, 32, 111
Quality control, 32, 111
Quality criteria, 166
Quality management plan, procuring outside
goods/services and, 138
Quality measures, 68
Quality plan, 29, A-3
    creating, 40
        action tool, 109–111
Quality policy, 110
Quality verification checklists, 109
Quantification, of risk, 131
Quotations, soliciting, 31

Recognition, 164
Recruiting, 122
Reporting process, 164
Reporting requirements, 113
Request for proposal, 42, 137, 141
Resource, defined, C-20
Resource allocation, B-3
Resource leveling, defined, C-20--C-21
Resource requirements, A-3
    action tool, 78–83
    authorization for, 60, 66

estimating, 39, 85
    risk and, 131
Resource-based duration, defined, C-20
Resources, procuring outside, 42, A-3
    action tool, 136–148
Response plans, action tool, 129–135
Responsibility/accountability matrix (illus.), 120
    worksheet (illus.), 124–126
Results. *See* Deliverables
Rewards, identifying, 164
Rework, 165
RFP. *See* Request for proposal
Risk
    assessment, 29
    control, 32
    identifying, 41, A-3
        action tool, 129–135
    project plan and, 151
    shortcuts for low-risk projects, A-1–A-4
Risk management plan, 129, 133
    review of, 168
    updating, 165

Schedule, 105, B-2
    action tool, 84–94
    criteria, 68
    developing, 29, 40, A-3
    management plan, 84
    reviewing, 167

Schedule finish date, defined, C-21
Schedule variance, defined, C-21
Scheduled start date, defined, C-21
Scheduling, defined, C-21
Scope, defined, C-22
Scope change, defined, C-22
Scripts, 6
Sequence, defined, C-22
Shortcuts, for low-risk projects, A-1–A-4
Slack, defined, C-22
Slack time, C-7, C-8
Slippage, defined, C-22
Software, 7
SOR. *See* Statement of requirements
SOW. *See* Statement of work
Specifications, creating, 14–16, 22, 48
Spending plan, 40, A-3
    action tool, 104–108
    creating, 40
Sponsors, 28
    approval of deliverables, 17
    approval of final product, 18
    approval of project, 59
    approval of project phase, 63
    approval of specifications, 16
    close-out and, 153
    defined, 57
    listing, 54, 55
    project plan review and, 154–155

Staff acquisition, 41, A-3
    action tool, 118–129
Staffing plan, 29, 41, 120–121
    review, 158
    risk and, 131
Stakeholders
    approval of deliverables, 17
    approval of final product, 18, 24
    approval of planning document, 14
    approval of project phase, 65
    approval of project plan, 21
    approval of specifications, 16
    close-out and, 153
    communications needs, 31, 113–114
    defined, 10, C-23
    listing, 54, 55
    project plan review and, 154–155
    risk identification and, 131
    roles, 71
Start date, schedule, C-21
Start float, defined, C-23
Starting activity, defined, C-23
Start-to-start lag, defined, C-23
Statement of requirements, 42, 136, 141
Statement of work, 42, 136, 141
    defined, C-23
Status reports, 168
Strategic value, B-1–B-2
Strategy definition, 13, 20

Sub-critical activity, defined, C-23–C-24
Subject-matter experts, 127–128, 140
Subnet, defined, C-24
Subnetwork, defined, C-24
Subproject, defined, C-24
Successor, defined, C-24
Super-critical activity, defined, C-24
System specifications, 6
Target finish—activity, defined, C-24–C-25
Target finish—project, defined, C-25
Target start—activity, defined, C-25
Task, defined, C-25
Team development, 31
Team performance assessment, 160
Testing, 9, 17–18, 24
    action tools, 49
    deliverables, 186
Text tables, 40, 84, (illus.) 93
Time-scaled network diagram, C-25
To do list, 166–169
Top down estimating, 96
Total float, defined, C-25–C-26
Training needs, 31, 122, 164

Unit price contracts, 148

Variable cost resources, 97
Variance, schedule, C-21
Variance analyzer, 172–174

Variances, 31–32
    analysis of, 167, 172–174
Vendors, 31
    estimates from, 136. *See also* Bids
    in-house vs. outside, 139

WBS. *See* Work breakdown structure
Work, defined, C-6
Work breakdown structure, 39, 67, 69, 74,
    75, 105, 151, 185
    defined, C-26
    example (illus.), 72–73
    risk and, 130
    updating, 165
Work flow, defined, C-26
Work load, defined, C-26
Work package, defined, C-27
Work results, 160
Work units, defined, C-26
Worksheets
    communications planner, 116–117
    deliverables status analyzer, 170–171
    duration of activities and resources
        estimate, 82–83
    phase authorization, 65–66
    project authorization, 59–60
    project charter, 61–62
    project issue tracker, 180–181
    project life cycle, 19–24
    project need and feasibility, 55–57

project scope, 70–71
project scope change order, 178–179
project status report, 182–183
risk assessment and response analyzer,
  134–135
sign-off form, 189–190
variance analyzer, 172–174

Zero float, defined, C-27